The Newbery and Caldecott Awards

A Guide to the
Medal and Honor Books

1992 Edition

Association for Library Service to Children

American Library Association
Chicago and London
1992

Cover design by Peter Broeksmit

Text design by Bottega Design Inc.

Desktop composition by Marie-Louise Settem on a Macintosh SE FD HD using Aldus PageMaker 4.0 software and output to a LaserWriter IINT printer

Printed on 50-pound Finch Opaque, an acid-free stock, and bound in 10-point Carolina cover stock by IPC, St. Joseph, Michigan

The paper used in this publication meets the minimum requirements of American National Standard for Information Sciences—Permanence of Paper for Printed Library Materials, ANSI Z39.48–1984. ∞

Cover art on p. 10 © 1991 Lynne Dennis; photo of the author courtesy of Atheneum. Cover art on p. 66 © 1991 David Wiesner; photo of the author courtesy of Clarion Books.

Library of Congress Cataloging-in-Publication Data

The Newbery and Caldecott awards : a guide to the medal and honor
   books / Association for Library Service to Children. – 1992 ed.
        p.   cm.
     Includes indexes.
     ISBN 0-8389-3411-0 (alk. paper)
     1. Bibliography--Best books--Children's literature.
   2. Illustrated books. Children's--United States--Awards.
   3. Children's literature. American–Bibliography. 4. Illustrated
   books, Children's--Bibliography. 5. Children's literature.
   American--Awards. 6. Caldecott medal books--Bibliography.
   7. Newbery medal books--Bibliography. 8. Literary prizes--United
   States. I. Association for Library Service to Children.
     Z1037.A2N474   1992
   [PN1009.A1]
     011'.62–dc20
                                                                   92-9250
                                                                      CIP

Printed in the United States of America.

96 95 94 93 92   5 4 3 2 1

To Christine Behrmann

Contents

Preface

The most frequently asked questions in the office of the Association for Library Service to Children have to do with the Newbery and Caldecott awards — an average of over one hundred calls a month. This 1992 edition of *The Newbery and Caldecott Awards* seeks to answer many of those questions. It serves as a guide to the books through lively annotations of all the medal and honor books.

We have updated the information on the media used in Caldecott Medal and Honor Books to keep it current. The original work was prepared by Christine Behrmann, former Children's Materials Specialist at the New York Public Library, for her article "The Media Used in Caldecott Picture Books: Notes toward a Definitive List," originally published in the *Journal of Youth Services in Libraries*, Winter, 1988. We will miss Christine Behrmann both personally and professionally, and we dedicate the 1992 edition to her memory.

Bette J. Peltola's "Newbery and Caldecott Medals: Authorization and Terms" is the prized essay for this edition. Peltola's discussion of the intricate terms and definitions that have evolved as both medals have become traditions in children's literature should prove insightful to most of our readers.

Finally, the inclusion of pictures of the medalists and remarks from the chairs of the 1992 committees when the medals were announced in January capture the excitement and enthusiasm conveyed by the committees in selecting these books.

The 1992 guide should be useful to you. We welcome suggestions for future editions.

The annotations for the 1992 edition were added to the basic ones prepared by Priscilla L. Drach, Children's Services Manager, and Barbara M. Barstow, Assistant Children's Services Manager, of the Cuyahoga County (Ohio) Public Library. Ms. Barstow is the past president of the Association for Library Service to Children.

Susan Roman
Executive Director
Association for Library Service
to Children

Another Look at Awards

Newbery and Caldecott Medals:
Authorization and Terms

Bette J. Peltola

Origins of the Medals

Each year the Newbery and Caldecott Medals are awarded by the American Library Association for the most distinguished American children's books published the previous year. On June 21, 1921, Frederic G. Melcher proposed to the American Library Association meeting of the Children's Librarians' Section that a medal be given for the most distinguished children's book of the year. He suggested that it be named for the eighteenth-century English bookseller John Newbery. The idea was enthusiastically accepted by the children's librarians, and Melcher's official proposal was approved by the ALA Executive Board in 1922. In Melcher's formal agreement with the board, the purpose of the Newbery Medal was stated as follows: "To encourage original and creative work in the field of books for children. To emphasize to the public that contributions to the literature for children deserve similar recognition to poetry, plays, or novels. To give those librarians, who make it their life work to serve children's reading interests, an opportunity to encourage good writing in this field."

The description of the award adopted in 1922 indicated that the Newbery Medal "is to be awarded annually to the author of the 'most distinguished contribution to American literature for children,' the award being made to cover books whose publication in book form falls in the calendar year last elapsed. The award is restricted to authors who are citizens or residents of the United States. Reprints and compilations are not eligible for consideration. There are no limitations as to the character of the book considered except that it be original work. It need not be written

Dr. Peltola is associate dean, School of Education, University of Wisconsin-Milwaukee.

solely for children[;] the judgment of the librarians voting shall decide whether a book be a 'contribution to the literature for children.' The award considers only the books of one calendar year and does not pass judgment on the author's previous work or other work during that year outside the volume that may be named." In 1932 the Section for Library Work with Children, with Melcher's approval, adopted the following: "To be eligible for the Newbery Medal books must be original, or, if traditional in origin, the result of individual research, the retelling and reinterpretation being the writer's own."

In 1937 Melcher suggested a second annual medal, this to be given to the artist who had created the most distinguished picture book of the year and to be called the Caldecott Medal in honor of Randolph J. Caldecott, the nineteenth-century English illustrator. The idea for this medal was also accepted enthusiastically by the Section for Library Work with Children of ALA and was approved by the ALA Executive Board.

The Caldecott Medal "shall be awarded to the artist of the most distinguished American Picture Book for Children published in the United States during the preceding year. The award shall go to the artist, who must be a citizen or resident of the United States, whether or not he be the author of the text. Members of the Newbery Medal Committee will serve as judges. If a book of the year is nominated for both the Newbery and Caldecott awards the committee shall decide under which heading it shall be voted upon, so that the same title shall not be considered on both ballots." In 1977 the Board of Directors of the Association for Library Service to Children rescinded the final part of the 1937 action and approved that "any book published in the preceding year shall be eligible to be considered for either award or both awards."

Changes in Terms

For the Caldecott Medal, additional qualifications for eligibility growing out of committee deliberations were defined over the years. The text need not be the work of the artist by must be worthy of the book. There is no limitation on age level of books to be considered, although it is recognized that most picture books are intended for young children. The award is made for a picture book in which the pictures rather than the text are the heart of the book.

A resolution by the Section for Library Work with Children in 1932 that "the book of a previous award winner shall receive the award only upon the unanimous vote" of the committee was later rescinded by the Children's Services Division Board of Directors. "In view of the fact that a unanimous vote in the case of a previous winner of the Newbery or Caldecott awards was first instituted to encourage new authors and illustrators at a period when such encouragement was needed and since such need is no longer apparent, the restriction of a unanimous vote for winning either award more than once [is] removed from terms for selection [of the awards]" (1958). In 1963 it was voted by the Children's Services Division that "joint authors shall be eligible" for the awards.

In 1978, the ALSC Board of Directors adopted new statements of terms, definitions, and criteria for each award. The new statements were prepared and adopted to provide further clarification of the basis on which the awards are to be given.

Newbery Award

The terms, definitions, and criteria for the Newbery Award are as follows:

Terms

1. The Medal shall be awarded annually to the author of the most distinguished contribution to American literature for children published in the United States during the preceding year. There are no limitations as to the character of the book considered except that it be original work.
2. The Award is restricted to authors who are citizens or residents of the United States.
3. The committee in its deliberations is to consider only the books eligible for the Award as specified in the terms.

Definitions

1. "*Contribution* to American *literature*" indicates the text of a book. It also implies that the committee shall consider all forms of writing—fiction, nonfiction, and poetry. Reprints and compilations are not eligible.
2. A "Contribution to American literature for *children*" shall be a book for which children are a potential audience. The book displays respect for children's understandings, abilities, and appreciations. "Children" are defined as persons of ages up to and including fourteen, and books for this entire age range are to be considered.
3. "Distinguished" is defined as:
   - marked by eminence and distinction: noted for significant achievement
   - marked by excellence in quality
   - marked by conspicuous excellence or eminence
   - individually distinct

4. "Author" may include coauthors. The author may be awarded the medal posthumously.
5. In defining the term "original work," the committee will consider books that are traditional in origin, if the book is the result of original research and the retelling and interpretation are the writer's own.
6. "American literature published in the United States" means that books originally published in other countries are not eligible.
7. "Published . . . during the preceding year" means that the book has a publication date in that year, was available for purchase in that year, and has a copyright date no later than that year. A book might have a copyright date prior to the year under consideration but, for various reasons, was not published until the year under consideration.
8. "Resident" specifies that the author has established and maintained residence in the United States as distinct from being a casual or occasional visitor.
9. The term "only the books eligible for the Award" specifies that the committee is not to consider the entire body of the work of an author or whether the author has previously won the award. The committee's decision is to be made following deliberations about the books of the specified calendar year.

Criteria

1. In identifying distinguished writing in a book for children:
   a. Committee members need to consider:
   Interpretation of the theme or concept.
   Presentation of information including accuracy, clarity and organization.
   Development of plot.
   Delineation of characters.
   Delineation of setting.
   Appropriateness of style.
   Note: Because the literary qualities to be considered will vary depending on content, the committee need not expect to find excellence in each of the named elements. The book should, however, have distinguished qualities in all of the elements pertinent to it.
   b. Committee members must not consider excellence of presentation for a child audience.
2. Each book is to be considered as a contribution to literature. The committee is to make its decision primarily on the text. Other aspects of a book are to be considered only if they distract from the text. Such other aspects might include illustrations, overall design of the book, etc.
   Note: The committee should keep in mind that the award is for literary quality and quality of presentation for children. The award is not for didactic intent or for popularity.

Caldecott Award
The terms, definitions, and criteria for the Caldecott Award are as follows:

Terms
1. The Medal shall be awarded annually to the artist of the most distinguished American picture book for children published in the United States during the preceding year. There are no limitations as to the character of the picture book except that the illustrations be original work.
2. The Award is restricted to artists who are citizens or residents of the United States.
3. The committee in its deliberations is to consider only the books eligible for the Award, as specified in the terms.

Definitions
1. A "picture book for children," as distinguished from other books with illustrations, is one that essentially provides the child with a visual experience. A picture book has a collective unity of story-line, theme, or concept, developed through the series of pictures of which the book is comprised.
2. A "picture book for children" is one for which children are a potential audience. The book displays respect for children's understandings, abilities, and appreciations. "Children" are defined as persons of ages up to and including fourteen, and picture books for this entire age range are to be considered.
3. "Distinguished" is defined as:
   • marked by eminence and distinction: noted for significant achievement
   • marked by excellence in quality
   • marked by conspicuous excellence or eminence
   • individually distinct
4. The "artist" is the illustrator or coillustrators. The artist may be awarded the Medal posthumously.
5. "Original work" means that illustrations reprinted or compiled from other sources are not eligible.
6. "American picture book published in the United States" specifies that books originally published in other countries are not eligible.
7. "Published . . . in the preceding year" means that the book has a publication date in that year, was available for purchase in that year, and has a copyright date no later than that year. A book might have a copyright date prior to the year under consideration but, for various reasons, was not published until the year under consideration.
8. "Resident" specifies that the artist has established and maintained residence in the United States as distinct from being a casual or occasional visitor.

9. The term "only the books eligible for the Award" specifies that the committee is not to consider the entire body of the work by an artist or whether the artist has previously won the award. The committee's decision is to be made following deliberation about the picture books of the specified calendar year.

Criteria

1. In identifying a distinguished picture book for children:
   a. Committee members need to consider:
   Excellence of execution in the artistic technique employed.
   Excellence of pictorial interpretation of story, theme, or concept; of appropriateness of style of illustration to the story, theme, or concept; of delineation of plot, theme, characters, setting, mood, or information through the pictures.
   b. Committee members must consider excellence of presentation in recognition of a child audience.
2. The only limitation to graphic form is that the form must be one which may be used in a picture book (e.g., motion-picture photography is not at present possible, though still photography is).
3. Each book is to be considered as a picture book. The committee is to make its decision primarily on the illustrations, but other components of a book are to be considered especially when they make a book less effective as a children's picture book. Such other components might include the written text, the overall design of the book, etc.
   Note: The committee should keep in mind that the award is for distinguished illustrations in a picture book and for excellence of pictorial presentation for children. The award is not for didactic intent or for popularity.

Changes in Committee Structure

In 1921 Melcher had the Newbery Medal designed by René Paul Chambellan. In 1937 Chambellan designed the Caldecott Medal. The ALA Executive Board in 1922 delegated to the Children's Librarians' Section the responsibility for selecting the book to receive the Newbery Medal. The inscription on the medal still reads "Children's Librarians' Section," although the section has changed its name four times and its membership now includes both school and public library children's librarians in contrast to the years 1922-58, when the section, under three different names, included only public library children's librarians. (The section names: until 1929, Children's Librarians' Section; 1929-42, Section for Library Work with Children; 1942-58, Children's Library Association; 1958-77, Children's Service Division; and, Association for Library Service to Children (ALSC), 1977 to date.

When the Caldecott Medal was accepted in 1937, the Section for Library Work with Children invited the School Libraries Section (now American Association of School Librarians) to name five of its members to the awards committee each year. For this reason the Caldecott Medal inscription reads: "Awarded annually by the Children's and School Librarians Sections of the American Library Association." This is a combination and simplification of the actual names of the sections. The wording continues even though several ALA reorganizations resulted in 1958 in the present divisions, among them the Children's Services Division (now the Association for Library Service to Children), made up of public library children's librarians, school librarians, and others interested in children's library services and good books for children. In 1958 the Children's Services Division Board of Directors recognized that the wording on both medals was incorrect in terms of current ALA terminology. It realized that confusion about the membership of the committee that chooses the medal winners could result from the discrepancies. However, the CSD board decided to request no change in the inscription on either medal, preferring to have them continue in their original form and design.

Honor Books

From the beginning of the awarding of the medals, committees could, and usually did, cite other books as worthy of attention. Such books were referred to as runners-up. In 1971 the term "runners-up," used to designate books cited with the annual Newbery and Caldecott medal winners, was changed to "honor books." The new terminology was made retroactive so that all runners-up are now referred to as Newbery or Caldecott Honor Books.

At the same meeting, the Board of Directors of the Children's Services Division also approved silver facsimile seals with the designation "Newbery Honor Book" and "Caldecott Honor Book," which may be placed on the honor books in similar fashion to the use made of the gold facsimile seals of the medals placed on the award-winning books. The gold and silver facsimile seals are sold by the Association for Library Service to Children, with all profits going to financially support the division's Frederic G. Melcher Scholarship Fund. Permission for photographic reproduction of the medals is also controlled by the association; profits from commercial reproduction also go to the Scholarship Fund.

In 1978 the ALSC board approved the presentation of certificates to the authors of the Newbery Honor Books and the illustrators of the Caldecott Honor Books.

Although some procedures have changed over the years the awards have been given, and some rules or aspects of what the awards are for have been clarified or modified, the basic purpose of honoring distinguished American children's books has not changed. Numerous committees have studied virtually every aspect of the award-giving procedure, the rationale, and the impact of the awards over the years. Such study is likely to continue and ensures a vital life to these awards that have had such an impact on the quality of American literature for children.

The Newbery Winners

1992–1922

SHILOH
Phyllis Reynolds Naylor

1992 Newbery Award

Shiloh. Phyllis Reynolds Naylor. Atheneum.

"In what appears to be a simple regional story of a boy trying to protect a dog, Naylor has created a poignant novel which at the same time explores the universal questions of honesty and commitment," said Pat Scales, Newbery Award Selection Committee chair. "All of the elements of distinguished fiction converge to make this a powerful book."

Naylor met the dog, who is Shiloh in this story, during a visit to West Virginia. She said it was the saddest dog she had ever seen. For weeks after returning home, Naylor said she could not get it out of her mind. And so she did what she always does when a problem haunts her—work it out in a book.

1992 Honor Books

Nothing but the Truth. Avi. Jackson/Orchard.

"Using a distinctive documentary format, Avi compels the reader to explore the issues of perception, reality, bias and expediency in his powerful *Nothing But the Truth*," said Scales. "From a small incident arising from the attitude of a student toward a teacher, the novel builds with compelling momentum toward a climax which holds no easy solutions."

The Wright Brothers: How They Invented the Airplane. Russell Freedman. Holiday House.

"Freedman seamlessly blends science, history and biography in his book *The Wright Brothers: How They Invented the Airplane*," said Scales. "Using Wilber and Orville Wright's own photographs as well as excerpts from their notes and journals, he has created a uniquely personal and engaging view of their accomplishments."

1991 AWARD   **Maniac Magee.** Jerry Spinelli. Little, Brown.
Jeffrey Lionel Magee is a legendary character who runs the rails faster than other kids run the ground. Jeffrey bunts "the world's first frogball for a four-bagger" and performs other amazing feats.

Honor   **The True Confessions of Charlotte Doyle.** Avi. Jackson/Orchard.
Avi weaves a finely crafted tale of high seas adventure and gripping suspense, made rich by 13-year-old Charlotte's deepening understanding of honor and herself.

1990 AWARD   **Number the Stars.** Lois Lowry. Houghton.
When ten-year-old Annemarie Johansen's family decides to pretend that her friend Ellen Rosen is her sister, they become involved in the effort to save the Danish Jews from the Nazis. As the author deftly portrays deep friendship, a strong family, and heroism in wartime, the story builds to a tense climax.

Honors   **Afternoon of the Elves.** Janet Taylor Lisle. Jackson/ Orchard.
Fascinated by Sarah-Kate's backyard elf village, Hillary is unprepared for the secret side of the older girl's life. Strong, tough, an outcast at school, Sarah-Kate has been doing whatever she must to care for herself and her mentally ill mother. When her plight is discovered by adults, disturbing but necessary changes occur.

The Winter Room. Gary Paulsen. Jackson/Orchard.
From the first page to the last, this story of farm life in northern Minnesota is so engrossing that the place and the people seem real. Eldon, the eleven-year-old narrator, takes the reader through the seasons and into the winter room, where stories are "not for believing so much, as to be believed in."

Shabanu, Daughter of the Wind. Suzanne Fisher Staples. Knopf.
Spirited and courageous Shabanu, younger daughter of present-day Pakistani camel herders, loves her family's life and her role in caring for their camels. Both Shabanu and her older sister are betrothed to brothers, but as her sister's wedding nears, a calamity occurs that changes forever the life of independent Shabanu.

1989 AWARD   **Joyful Noise: Poems for Two Voices.** Paul Fleischman. Illustrated by Eric Beddows. Zolotow/Harper.

Fourteen poems, using two voices, sometimes alternating, sometimes together, offer listeners a look at what insects just might think of themselves and their world. The book lice, grasshoppers, house crickets, and their poetic companions are illustrated in soft yet often comical black-and-white pencil drawings.

Honors   **In the Beginning: Creation Stories from Around the World.** Virginia Hamilton. Illustrated by Barry Moser. Harcourt.

Stories from African, Chinese, Native American, and Guinean peoples are represented among the twenty-five creation myths found in this collection. Faithfully retold, the stories are followed by notes about their sources. Dramatic watercolor paintings accent each tale.

Scorpions. Walter Dean Myers. Harper.
Hoping to find a way to raise money for an appeal for his imprisoned older brother, twelve-year-old Jamal agrees to try to become the leader of his brother's Harlem gang, the Scorpions. Involvement with the gang (and the gun he is given) leads to tragedy for Jamal and his friend Tito.

1988 AWARD   **Lincoln: A Photobiography.** Russell Freedman. Clarion.

An ambitious man, Lincoln struggled hard to get an education, to build his law practice, and to become politically successful. The man, his wit, and his wisdom are vividly and honestly portrayed in this straightforward biography and its ninety photographs.

Honors   **After the Rain.** Norma Fox Mazer. Morrow.
Fifteen-year-old Rachel tries to balance her concern for her own life with her grandfather's need for her help. Never close to the old man, she slowly comes to love him. As she struggles to help him maintain his independence, he weakens and nears death.

Hatchet. Gary Paulsen. Bradbury.
When the pilot dies of a heart attack, Brian crash-lands the small plane in the Canadian wilderness. Left with only a hatchet and the clothes he is wearing, Brian begins a gripping fifty-four-day ordeal that challenges his physical and psychological skills to their limits.

1987 AWARD **The Whipping Boy.** Sid Fleischman. Illustrated by Peter Sis. Greenwillow.

Whenever Prince Brat does anything bad, Jemmy, his whipping boy, is punished. The spoiled prince decides to run away from the palace, forcing Jemmy to go with him. Far from the safety of the court, the prince quickly learns how little he knows about the outside world and how important Jemmy is to his survival.

Honors **On My Honor.** Marion Dane Bauer. Clarion.
Before leaving on a bike ride with his impetuous friend Tony, Joel gives his father his word of honor that he will not swim in a river known to be dangerous. Tony convinces Joel that the river is safe; the two swim; and Tony drowns. Joel is left alone to face his guilt, both sets of parents, and his own grief.

Volcano: The Eruption and Healing of Mount St. Helens. Patricia Lauber. Bradbury.
The eruption of Mount St. Helens and the subsequent regrowth of plants are vividly portrayed in color photographs and a dynamic text. The volcanic eruption is seen not as just a disaster, but as a builder of life on this planet.

A Fine White Dust. Cynthia Rylant. Bradbury.
Although neither his parents nor his best friend are particularly religious, Peter feels a need for something deeper than just churchgoing. When an itinerant preacher comes to town, Peter is mesmerized by the man and "saved." Invited to go away with the preacher, Peter reluctantly agrees, only to be left behind and forgotten.

1986 AWARD **Sarah, Plain and Tall.** Patricia MacLachlan. Zolotow/Harper.

Life on the prairie with two children and no wife is lonely and difficult, so Caleb and Anna's father advertises for a wife. Sarah answers his ad and soon agrees to come all the way from Maine for a visit. Captivated by her, Anna and Caleb worry that Sarah misses the sea too much to stay with them.

Honors **Commodore Perry in the Land of the Shogun.** Rhoda Blumberg. Lothrop.
Commodore Perry's fascinating mission to Japan in 1853 is told at a lively pace, with special attention given to the

negotiating skill that led to his success; to his sensitivity to cultural differences; and to his just plain curiosity. The accompanying pictures include many sketched by the Japanese and the Americans who were with Matthew Perry.

Dogsong. Gary Paulsen. Bradbury.
Unhappy with the snowmobile-and-television society that seems to have taken over his Eskimo village, Russell turns to Oogruk, the old man of the village, for help in finding a path back to the old ways. With Oogruk's advice and encouragement, Russell begins an arduous dogsled journey northward to find his own "song."

1985 AWARD

The Hero and the Crown. Robin McKinley. Greenwillow.
The daughter of the king of Damar and his second wife (a witch woman from the north), Aerin does not fit in at court. Unable to succeed her father to the throne, she must instead find her own destiny. Wielding her blue sword, she not only defeats dragons but finally becomes the hero of the kingdom.

Honors

The Moves Make the Man. Bruce Brooks. Harper.
The first black to go to the formerly all-white junior high school, Jerome is a passionate basketball player. When he meets Bix Rivers, an unstable outsider who is a gifted athlete, Jerome decides to teach him basketball. As they play the game, Bix's mental illness becomes more apparent, and Jerome is less able to help him.

One-Eyed Cat. Paula Fox. Bradbury.
After his minister father takes his new air rifle away from him and puts it in the attic, Ned sneaks upstairs, takes it, fires it once, and is terrified that he may have hit a cat. Struggling with his guilt, he tells one lie after another until he cannot bear it anymore and must confess to someone.

Like Jake and Me. Mavis Jukes. Illustrated by Lloyd Bloom. Knopf.
Alex wants to be liked by his rugged cowboy stepfather, but there are still barriers between the two. When Alex notices a wolf spider on Jake's neck and calmly mentions it, the rugged cowboy totally panics, admitting his terror of spiders. Alex comes to the rescue, and the two finally come to appreciate each other and their differences.

1984 AWARD

Dear Mr. Henshaw. Beverly Cleary. Illustrated by Paul O. Zelinsky. Morrow.

Leigh Botts starts writing to the author of *Ways to Amuse a Dog* in second grade. Year after year the letters, and then a diary, become vehicles for expressing his feelings about himself, his parents' divorce, and his problems in school. Leigh's growth and acceptance of the divorce are tempered with much humor.

Honors

The Wish Giver: Three Tales of Coven Tree. Bill Brittain. Illustrated by Andrew Glass. Harper.

Thaddeus Blinn, the wish giver, sells Polly, Rowena, Henry, and Stew Meat wishes. All they have to do is hold the white card with the dot and wish carefully. The first three make their wishes with dire but comical consequences and leave Stew Meat to use his to undo everything they have done.

Sugaring Time. Kathryn Lasky. Photographs by Christopher G. Knight. Macmillan.

The author and photographer record a family's old-fashioned method of sugaring. When the right time finally comes, family members tap the maple trees, boil the sap, and enjoy a sugar-on-snow party and a pancake breakfast. The family's enjoyment of sugaring is evident in the often poetic text and the clear black-and-white photographs.

The Sign of the Beaver. Elizabeth George Speare. Houghton.

Left alone in the Maine wilderness, Matt first loses his rifle and food and then is savagely stung by bees. Found by Saknis, chief of the Beaver tribe, Matt is cared for in exchange for teaching the chief's grandson to read. As the boys' friendship develops, Matt gains an appreciation for the heritage and skills of the Beaver tribe.

A Solitary Blue. Cynthia Voigt. Atheneum.

Abandoned at the age of seven by his cause-conscious mother, Jeff is left to fend for himself and take care of his absent-minded-professor father. Not until Jeff is stricken with pneumonia at the age of twelve does his father understand how he, too, has deserted his son. Slowly the two build a close, strong relationship that is able to help them survive and grow.

1983 AWARD

Dicey's Song. Cynthia Voigt. Atheneum.

Finally settled in with Gram Tillerman while their mother is in a mental hospital, Dicey and her brothers and sisters discover that it is not easy to become a family. They must learn to love and trust Gram — and she them — while they try to adjust to a new school and make friends.

Honors
Graven Images. Paul Fleischman. Illustrated by Andrew Glass. Harper.
Three gripping stories, two sinister and one funny and all with historical settings, are centered on graven images: a wooden boy with a frightening secret, a weathervane that leads to true love, and a statue ordered by a ghost.

Homesick: My Own Story. Jean Fritz. Illustrated by Margot Tomes. Putnam.
Fritz remembers with humor and poignancy two years of her childhood in China during the turbulent 1920s. She contends with being a "foreign devil," losing a longed-for baby sister, and, most of all, longing for the United States, a country she has never seen.

Sweet Whispers, Brother Rush. Virginia Hamilton. Philomel.
Life changes radically for fourteen-year-old Tree and her older retarded brother when the ghost of Brother Rush appears to Tree, first in the street and then in her home. The handsome ghost of her mother's brother takes her back in time to bear witness to the past and to learn about the terrible disease that is killing her own brother.

The Blue Sword. Robin McKinley. Greenwillow.
Angharad Crewe is yanked out of an easy life on a Homelander outpost and thrust into one of rigorous training for her prophesied role as deliverer of the Hillfolk. She earns the right to carry the Blue Sword into battle, and with it she heroically leads a small band of warriors against the nonhuman Northerners.

Doctor De Soto. William Steig. Farrar.
As mice dentists, the diminutive De Sotos have always refused to treat dangerous animals until a miserable fox appears begging for help. The compassionate mice cleverly find a way to rid the fox of his pain while guaranteeing their own safety.

1982 AWARD
A Visit to William Blake's Inn: Poems for Innocent and Experienced Travelers. Nancy Willard. Illustrated by Alice and Martin Provensen. Harcourt.

Written in the spirit of William Blake, these magical poems are built around the visit of a child to Blake's inn. It is staffed by mighty dragons that brew and bake, angels that wash feather beds, and animals that dance to the music of the Marmalade Man.

Honors	**Ramona Quimby, Age 8.** Beverly Cleary. Illustrated by Alan Tiegreen. Morrow.

Ramona is now starting the third grade and her life is full of the usual hilarious trials that cause her to be labelled a "nuisance and show-off" by her new teacher. Whether she is deciding she prefers her printed *Q* to the floppy cursive one, getting raw egg in her hair, or facing an interminably boring Sunday, Ramona is always a memorable character.

Upon the Head of the Goat: A Childhood in Hungary 1939–1944. Aranka Siegal. Farrar.

The destruction of nine-year-old Piri's family begins with Hungary's occupation by the Nazis. Her mother valiantly tries to keep the family together and safe, but one loss after another occurs until they board trains that will take them to Auschwitz. Siegal's book is a powerful autobiography.

1981 AWARD — **Jacob Have I Loved.** Katherine Paterson. Crowell.

Although she takes pride in her twin sister's singing talent, Wheeze (Louise) is jealous of the attention Caroline gets on their Chesapeake Bay island. It is only when she leaves and starts a life as a midwife in Kentucky that Wheeze comes to understand that she has always been loved and accepted for herself.

Honors — **The Fledgling.** Jane Langton. Illustrated by Erik Blegvad. Harper.

Frail young Georgie, almost light enough to blow away, is obsessed with her belief that she can fly. When a large Canada goose she has befriended hoots outside her window, Georgie hops on his back and flies away. Night after night they soar above Walden Pond until one misfortune and then another end Georgie's flying forever.

A Ring of Endless Light. Madeleine L'Engle. Farrar.
Sixteen-year-old Vicky and her family spend the summer on a New England island with her dying grandfather. All summer long she and her family are preoccupied with the mysteries of life, death, and eternity, yet there is still time for Vicky to help with a Marine Biology Station dolphin project and to date two boys.

1980 AWARD — **A Gathering of Days: A New England Girl's Journal, 1830–1832.** Joan W. Blos. Scribner.

Catherine Cabot Hall sporadically writes in her journal, filling it with recipes, excerpts from her copy book, secrets, fears, confidences, details of her adjustment to her stepmother, and thoughts on the pain of a friend's death. Though fiction, the journal is believable, and Catherine is easy to like.

Honor **The Road from Home: The Story of an Armenian Girl.** David Kherdian. Greenwillow.
After the Turks finish with their slaughter of nearly two million Armenians, Veron is the only survivor of her immediate family. When the Greeks attack Turkey, Veron and her aunt and cousin escape to Greece, and from there she travels to the United States, a mail-order bride and the future mother of the author.

1979 AWARD **The Westing Game.** Ellen Raskin. Dutton.
An expensive apartment building mysteriously fills up with sixteen occupants — all named as heirs or possible murderers in millionaire Sam Westing's will. The sixteen are paired, given $10,000, and challenged to discover who really killed Sam Westing.

Honor **The Great Gilly Hopkins.** Katherine Paterson. Crowell.
Abandoned as a preschooler, Gilly has gone through a succession of foster homes. Smart, self-sufficient, and superficially hard, Gilly manages to do just what she wants until she is sent to stay with Maime Trotter, a woman with a big heart, patience, and wisdom enough to know how to reach the unhappy girl.

1978 AWARD **Bridge to Terabithia.** Katherine Paterson. Illustrated by Donna Diamond. Crowell.
After practicing all summer to be the fastest runner in school, Jess is beaten by the new girl, Leslie. Gradually the two become close friends, creating an imaginary world in the wood and calling it Terabithia. When tragedy strikes, Jess, shocked and despairing, slowly begins to see the wonders Leslie left him.

Honors **Ramona and Her Father.** Beverly Cleary. Illustrated by Alan Tiegreen. Morrow.
Ramona is in second grade when her father loses his job and her mother begins to work full-time. Ramona tries her best to help her family through the crisis, even starting a campaign to get her father to quit smoking. Her worries, problems, and joys, presented with lively good humor, are common to many children her age.

Anpao: An American Indian Odyssey. Jamake Highwater. Illustrated by Fritz Scholder. Lippincott.
A beautiful Indian maiden promises to marry Anpao, but first he must get the Sun's permission and have him remove the ugly scar on his face. As Anpao travels the world looking for the Sun, he hears stories about his own roots as well as legends and myths of his people.

1977 AWARD

Roll of Thunder, Hear My Cry. Mildred D. Taylor. Dial.
Cassie Logan and her brothers are part of a warm, intelligent, and courageous black family in rural Mississippi during the Depression. They try to maintain their pride as they take abuse from white children and then recognize that their personal difficulties are only symptoms of greater problems within their community.

Honors

A String in the Harp. Nancy Bond. Atheneum.
Their father's remoteness and the strangeness of school in Wales make the children's adjustment to their mother's death even more difficult. Then twelve-year-old Peter finds an ancient harp key that pulls him back into Welsh history, helping him discover a purpose to living.

Abel's Island. William Steig. Farrar.
After a violent storm, Abel, a mouse, finds himself alone, bewildered, and far, far away from his beloved wife Amanda. Sustained by his love for his wife, Abel uses all his resources to survive for a year on the deserted island.

1976 AWARD

The Grey King. Susan Cooper. Illustrated by Michael Heslop. McElderry/Atheneum.
In Wales recovering from a serious illness, eleven-year-old Will, the youngest of the Old Ones, uses his considerable powers to find the golden harp that will awaken the Sleepers. It is not an easy quest, and Will has only the mysterious Bran and Bran's dog, Cafall, to help him fight the forces of dark and evil.

Honors

The Hundred Penny Box. Sharon Bell Mathis. Illustrated by Leo and Diane Dillon. Viking.
For each of her hundred years there is a penny in Aunt Dew's box and a story to go along with it. More than his parents, Michael understands the importance of the box to the old woman and loves to hear her tell the stories again and again.

Dragonwings. Laurence Yep. Harper.
In 1903 Moonshadow leaves the Middle Kingdom to join his father in San Francisco. To make the father's dream of building an aeroplane come true, the two of them leave the close-knit community that shelters their Chinese culture to live among white demons. Humorous accommodations are made between the different cultures as they grow in understanding and friendship.

1975 AWARD

M. C. Higgins, the Great. Virginia Hamilton. Macmillan.
Up on Sarah's Mountain, M. C. dreams of a way for his family to escape the spoil heap that may one day destroy their home. It is not his dreams but the boy's own strength and determination that help the family find a way to keep themselves safe.

Honors

My Brother Sam Is Dead. James Lincoln Collier and
    Christopher Collier. Four Winds.
Tim's older brother, Sam, defies their father and runs off to join the Continental Army. When their father is imprisoned by the rebels and dies and Sam is hung by his own army, Tim sees how devastating war can be.

Philip Hall Likes Me, I Reckon Maybe. Bette Greene.
    Illustrated by Charles Lilly. Dial.
Eleven-year-old Beth Lambert, a spunky heroine, realizes she has been letting Philip Hall be number one in school because she is afraid he will not like her if she surpasses him. With gentle prodding from her family, Beth decides to go ahead and do her best — even if it means beating Philip Hall.

The Perilous Gard. Elizabeth Marie Pope. Illustrated by
    Richard Cuffari. Houghton.
Banished by Queen Mary to the remote castle of Elvenwood, Kate Sutton quickly learns the castle's secret: It guards the last practitioners of the old religions. To keep their power, the fairy folk decide to sacrifice the man Kate loves on All Hallow's Eve.

Figgs & Phantoms. Ellen Raskin. Dutton.
Mona is embarrassed by her zany, ex–show business family — except for her four-foot-four-inch-tall Uncle Florence Italy Figg. When he dies, Mona is desolate. She is sure he has gone to Capri, the Figg family Heaven, and decides to follow him.

1974 AWARD   **The Slave Dancer.** Paula Fox. Illustrated by Eros
Keith. Bradbury.

Kidnapped and forced to play his fife while the slaves
"dance," thirteen-year-old Jessie learns all too soon about the
savagery of the slave trade. For four long months he lives
with the crew's cruelty until a storm wrecks the ship and
Jessie and Ras, a would-be slave, are the only survivors.

Honor   **The Dark Is Rising.** Susan Cooper. Illustrated by Alan
Cober. McElderry/Atheneum.
On midwinter's eve, Will's eleventh birthday, the world is in
turmoil with strange creatures appearing and stranger
things happening. Will, the last of the Old Ones to be born,
must use all his knowledge and skill to help in the fight
against the Dark.

1973 AWARD   **Julie of the Wolves.** Jean Craighead George.
Illustrated by John Schoenherr. Harper.

Having run away from a forced marriage, thirteen-year-old
Miyax, an Eskimo, becomes lost on the Arctic plain. Her
only hope for survival is acceptance by a wolf pack. Imitating their facial expressions and body movements, Miyax
slowly becomes one of them, while still trying to get to safety.

Honors   **Frog and Toad Together.** Arnold Lobel. Harper.
Whether they are testing their willpower with a bowl of
cookies or their patience while waiting for seeds to grow,
Frog and Toad delight in each other's company. Witty, easy-
to-read, and full of warmth and gentle humor, these five
stories engagingly explore the meaning of friendship.

The Upstairs Room. Johanna Reiss. Crowell.
As the German occupation of Holland tightens, two Jewish
sisters are forced to hide in a secret upstairs room in an old
farmhouse for two years. The girls experience fear, hope,
terror, and boredom in their daily life and depend on the
kindness and courage of others for their survival.

The Witches of Worm. Zilpha Keatley Snyder. Illustrated
by Alton Raible. Atheneum.
Deserted by her friends and her mother, Jessica channels her
anger at life into "evil acts" that her cat, Worm, supposedly
forces her to perform. Convinced first that Worm is a
witch's cat, then that she is a witch, Jessica is ultimately
forced to face herself and her feelings.

1972 AWARD

Mrs. Frisby and the Rats of NIMH. Robert C. O'Brien. Illustrated by Zena Bernstein. Atheneum.

When nothing she does seems to help her son Timothy get well, Mrs. Frisby, a widowed mouse, turns to a colony of super-intelligent rats for help. The rats' high intelligence is the result of experiments performed upon them by human scientists at NIMH. Now the rats are intent upon starting a new civilization free from human interference.

Honors

Incident at Hawk's Hill. Allan W. Eckert. Illustrated by John Schoenherr. Little, Brown.

Lonely, small, and frail, six-year-old Ben shies away from people but shows deep interest in and affinity toward animals. Lost during a storm, he takes refuge with a badger who has just lost her young. The badger adopts him, and he lives a feral life for three months until he is found. Convincingly written, the incident is based on an actual occurrence in 1870.

The Planet of Junior Brown. Virginia Hamilton. Macmillan.

For more than two months, huge, musical genius Junior Brown and his friend and protector Buddy Clark have been cutting classes and hiding in a secret basement room created by the school custodian. Buddy and Mr. Poole, the custodian, are trying desperately to help Junior, who seems to be slipping slowly but inexorably into madness.

The Tombs of Atuan. Ursula K. LeGuin. Illustrated by Gail Garraty. Atheneum.

From the time Tenar was five, her life has been focused on the tombs and her future as their priestess. Renamed Arha, she guards the labyrinthine tunnels, knowing that they hide great treasure. When she finds a man (Ged of *A Wizard of Earthsea*) in the tunnels seeking the other half to the Ring of Erreth-Akbe, Arha is torn between her duty to kill him and her compassion for him.

Annie and the Old One. Miska Miles. Illustrated by Peter Parnall. Little, Brown.

Annie likes her life the way it is with her mother weaving, her father making jewelry, and her grandmother, the Old One, always there to tell her stories and to help with chores. When grandmother announces that she will die when the new rug is finished, Annie tries desperately to stop the inevitable by secretly unravelling the rug.

The Headless Cupid. Zilpha Keatley Snyder. Illustrated by Alton Raible. Atheneum.

Eleven-year-old David is pleased about his father's remarriage until he meets his new stepsister, Amanda, a self-proclaimed witch. Angry at her mother for remarrying, Amanda sets up situations that lead the other children to believe their house is haunted. Then unexplained events turn the tables, frightening even Amanda.

1971 AWARD

Summer of the Swans. Betsy Byars. Illustrated by Ted CoConis. Viking.

An insecure fourteen-year-old, Sarah is unhappy with herself and her family. Though she loves her mentally disabled brother Charlie, Sarah is tired of always being responsible for him. When Charlie turns up missing, however, Sarah tries desperately to find him and in the process discovers that she is less the ugly duckling than she had supposed.

Honors

Knee Knock Rise. Natalie Babbitt. Farrar.

In this tale filled with folk humor, Egan goes to the village for a visit and becomes intrigued with the tales and wails of a monster that lives in the peaks of Knee Knock Rise. After an unprecedented climb up the mountain, Egan discovers the practical explanation for the legendary creature. The villagers refuse to listen to him, preferring to let their folklore live on as history.

Enchantress from the Stars. Sylvia Louise Engdahl. Illustrated by Rodney Shackell. Atheneum.

Invaded by technologically advanced Imperials, the Andrecians are close to being destroyed by their occupiers when beings from an even more highly advanced civilization decide to intervene secretly. Using their telekenetic powers, three Federation members pose as magicians, teaching a young Andrecian how to use his psychic abilities to combat the invaders.

Sing Down the Moon. Scott O'Dell. Houghton.

At fourteen, Bright Morning dares to be optimistic about her future. Her mother is a wealthy Navajo, and Bright Morning is to marry Tall Boy, a young Navajo warrior. Then she is wrenched from her home by Spanish slavers. When freed, she is uprooted again, this time by the cavalry, who force the Navajo to make a 300-mile march to Bosque Redondo.

1970 AWARD **Sounder.** William H. Armstrong. Illustrated by James Barkley. Harper.

Sounder, the family dog, valiantly defends the father when the sheriff and his deputies come to arrest him for stealing food for his starving family. Years later, the dog, shot and maimed by the deputies, is the only one to recognize the father when he returns, paralyzed and deformed.

Honors **Our Eddie.** Sulamith Ish-Kishor. Pantheon.

Eddie's father is a stern, insensitive zealot who refuses, until it is too late, to see that his son is gradually succumbing to a debilitating disease. Set in London and New York in the 1920s, most of this story of a warm Jewish immigrant family is told by Eddie's insightful sister.

The Many Ways of Seeing: An Introduction to the Pleasures of Art. Janet Gaylord Moore. Illustrated with black-and-white and color reproductions and photographs. World.

Moore, of the Cleveland Museum of Art, encourages readers to try a new way of approaching art: to see art reflecting the world and nature, and the world in turn reflecting art. Paintings (reproduced in color), poems, and quotations are arranged to lead to the discovery of new comparisons between modern, traditional, or ancient art and the imagery of word and picture.

Journey Outside. Mary Q. Steele. Illustrated by Rocco Negri. Viking.

In a story filled with allegory and symbolism, Dilar's people endlessly travel an underground river, headed for the "better place." But Dilar, suspecting that they are merely going around in circles, jumps from his raft and accidentally makes his way into the outside world. There, nearly blinded by the light, he tries to learn more about his people and to find a way to bring them aboveground.

1969 AWARD **The High King.** Lloyd Alexander. Holt.

In the final book of the chronicles of Prydain, Taran leads his forces against Arawn and his army of the dead. Victorious, but with great loss of life and destruction to Prydain, Taran becomes High King, fulfilling the predictions of his wizard guardian, Dallben.

Honors **To Be a Slave.** Julius Lester. Illustrated by Tom Feelings. Dial.

American slaves, runaways, and emancipated people provide a powerful testament of how they felt about slavery and what they endured. The author dynamically blends quotations from published and unpublished sources and presents them in rough chronological order.

When Shlemiel Went to Warsaw and Other Stories.
Isaac Bashevis Singer. Illustrated by Margot Zemach. Farrar.

In eight delightfully silly stories, five retold from the Yiddish and three original, readers are introduced to a memorable collection of characters. Among them are a mixed-up Shlemiel, who does not recognize his wife and village, and Utzel's daughter, Poverty, who seems to grow larger as he grows poorer.

1968 AWARD

From the Mixed-Up Files of Mrs. Basil E. Frankweiler. E. L. Konigsburg. Atheneum.

Having carefully planned how and to where they will run away, Claudia and her little brother, James (and his money), board a bus, head to New York City, and go to the Metropolitan Museum of Art. There they hide in washrooms, sleep on ancient beds, and get involved in solving an exciting mystery.

Honors

Jennifer, Hecate, Macbeth, William McKinley, and Me, Elizabeth. E. L. Konigsburg. Atheneum.

Elizabeth is lonely at her new school until she meets Jennifer, a girl her age who claims to be a real witch. In awe of Jennifer, Elizabeth agrees to become her apprentice and initially finds her boring life full of adventure. But Jennifer is very demanding, and even superficially docile Elizabeth can only be pushed so far.

The Black Pearl. Scott O'Dell. Illustrated by Milton Johnson. Houghton.

In this story written with stark simplicity and riveting suspense, Ramon confronts his two greatest enemies in the waters of Baja California. The legendary curse of the Manta Diablo holds true when Ramon wrests the fabulous black pearl from the Manta's cave and his life is changed forever.

The Fearsome Inn. Isaac Bashevis Singer. Illustrated by Nonny Hogrogian. Scribner.

Unaware that the owners of the inn are a witch and her half-devil husband, three young men seek shelter there on a stormy winter night. One of the three, a clever student of the Cabala, recognizes the couple's evil and courageously defeats them, sending the pair "behind the Mountains of Darkness where there is neither day nor night."

The Egypt Game. Zilpha Keatley Snyder. Illustrated by Alton Raible. Atheneum.
April and Melanie begin the Egypt game in the backyard of a slightly sinister curio shop. With costumes, ceremonies, an evil god, an oracular owl, and four other members, the game is seriously and imaginatively played. After the murder of a child, they are forced inside for awhile, but finally they begin the game again. This time one of the players almost becomes the next victim.

1967 AWARD **Up a Road Slowly.** Irene Hunt. Follett.

When Julie is seven, her mother dies. She and her little brother are sent to live with her strict, schoolteacher aunt. Through the years, Julie keeps hoping that her father will want them back, that staying with Aunt Cordelia is just temporary, but slowly she comes to love her aunt and wants to stay.

Honors **The King's Fifth.** Scott O'Dell. Illustrated by Samuel Bryant. Houghton.

Imprisoned in Vera Cruz and awaiting trial, seventeen-year-old Esteban tells of his part in the disastrous expedition for gold to the Seven Cities of Cibola. A mapmaker, Esteban is left with the bags of gold. After seeing the greed, cruelty, and, finally, death of those searching for it, he throws the gold into a volcanic crater.

Zlateh the Goat and Other Stories. Isaac Bashevis Singer. Illustrated by Maurice Sendak. Harper.
Seven stories rich with eastern European culture and Jewish folklore are filled with lively characters, delightfully funny fools, clever people, and loyal animals. The ink drawings of Sendak create wonderful scenes complementing the stories perfectly.

The Jazz Man. Mary Hays Weik. Illustrated by Ann Grifalconi. Atheneum.
Night after night Zeke and his mother and father listen to the jazz man play his piano. Then his mother tires of his father not working, and she leaves them. Soon his father goes as well, and Zeke is alone. As the gloomy days and nights pass, Zeke dreams of the jazz man and of better, happier times.

1966 AWARD **I, Juan de Pareja.** Elizabeth Borton de Trevino. Farrar.

Behind the great painter Velasquez stands his faithful slave, Juan, ready to prepare a canvas, mix paint, and boost his morale. But, secretly, Juan teaches himself to paint, winning his freedom and the respect of a great master.

Honors
The Black Cauldron. Lloyd Alexander. Holt.
Assistant Pig-Keeper Taran excitedly joins Gwydion and the other men of Prydain in their attack on Arawn, Lord of Annuvin, and his cauldron-born army. Only by destroying the cauldron can they hope to stop Arawn and his deathless warriors from overrunning Prydain.

The Animal Family. Randall Jarrell. Illustrated by Maurice Sendak. Pantheon.
Isolated in his house by the sea, the hunter is lonely until the day he sees the mermaid. Together they form an amazing family with first a bear cub, then a lynx, and finally an orphaned boy. Each fits gently and beautifully into the very special world created by the unusual couple.

The Noonday Friends. Mary Stolz. Illustrated by Louis Glanzman. Harper.
Her hard-working mother and out-of-work father depend on Franny to take care of her little brother after school and to help out in other ways. The only time left for friendship is during lunch hour at school when she talks to Simone, a friend with whom she can share problems.

1965 AWARD
Shadow of a Bull. Maia Wojciechowska. Illustrated by Alvin Smith. Atheneum.

With everyone waiting for him to become a great bullfighter like his father, Manolo is afraid to let them know that he has a different dream — to become a doctor. He trains and practices for the ring until finally he has the courage and confidence to admit that he can never be a bullfighter.

Honor
Across Five Aprils. Irene Hunt. Follett.
At nine, Jethro is excited by the prospect of a civil war coming to the country. When the nation really does go to war, his brothers and friends go in different directions, fighting for either the North or the South. Jethro begins to understand how devastating war really is to family and nation.

1964 AWARD
It's Like This, Cat. Emily Neville. Illustrated by Emil Weiss. Harper.

When his father suggests that owning a dog might be good for him, fourteen-year-old Dave defiantly goes to Aunt Kate the Cat Woman and adopts a stray. The cat ends up leading

him to new people and adventures all over Manhattan —
and even to an appreciation for his parents.

Honors   **Rascal: A Memoir of a Better Era.** Sterling North.
　　　Illustrated by John Schoenherr. Dutton.
For twelve months Sterling owned the raccoon, raising him
from a tiny captured kit to a large adult yearning for his
freedom. Bright, curious, energetic, and endearing, Rascal
fills the boy's life with love, companionship, and adventure
during their year together.

The Loner. Ester Wier. Illustrated by Christine Price. McKay.
Both nameless and homeless, the boy wanders the country
with other migrants, hoping to find work and food. Finally,
lost and weak from hunger, he collapses and is found by a
woman called The Boss. The gruff but gentle sheep rancher
names him David and gives him a chance to make his own
life on her Montana ranch.

1963 AWARD   **A Wrinkle in Time.** Madeleine L'Engle. Farrar.

Meg, Charles Wallace, and next-door neighbor Calvin go
into space and through time to rescue Meg's father, a
scientist who disappeared while working on a secret project.
The children's intergalactic search leads them to a confronta-
tion with the forces of evil on the planet Camazotz, where
conformity means survival.

Honors   **Thistle and Thyme: Tales and Legends from Scotland.**
　　　Sorche Nic Leodhas, pseud. (Leclaire Alger). Illustrated
　　　by Evaline Ness. Holt.
Using her memories of stories told in her family, the author
retells ten stories based on Scottish legends and folktales.
Some are humorous, others mysterious and suspenseful, and
all of them possess the rhythm of the Gaelic language.

Men of Athens. Olivia Coolidge. Illustrated by Milton
　　　Johnson. Houghton.
The golden age of Greece comes to life through the men and
women who lived during and immediately before and after
that brief fifty-year period. The battles they waged to make
Greece strong and free; the brilliance of the leading artists,
philosophers, and statesmen; and the excitement of the time
make exciting reading.

1962 AWARD   **The Bronze Bow.** Elizabeth George Speare. Houghton.

At the death of his parents, Daniel swears vengeance against
the Roman invaders. For five years he hides in the moun-

tains of Galilee with a band of rebels but finally must return to care for his sister. He meets Jesus but refuses to accept his message of love, wanting revenge instead. Only when all seems nearly lost does he start to understand the power of love.

Honors   **Frontier Living.** Edwin Tunis. World.
Beginning with the settlement of the Piedmont area in the early 1700s, nineteen distinct frontier movements take American settlers from the East Coast across the continent and through the nineteenth century. Details of daily life and carefully drawn pictures of the people and objects show what makes this era unique.

The Golden Goblet. Eloise Jarvis McGraw. Coward.
Under the control of his cruel and unscrupulous half-brother, Gebu, Ranofer, a boy of ancient Egypt who lives in Thebes, is sent to work for a goldsmith. Slowly he discovers that Gebu is stealing gold objects from the Valley of the Tombs, and he must find a way to expose him.

Belling the Tiger. Mary Stolz. Illustrated by Beni Montresor. Harper.
Asa and Rambo, the two smallest mice, are given the dubious honor of belling the cat. While getting the bell, the two accidentally get stuck on a ship and travel to a tropical island where they "bell" a tiger. Home again, the diminutive duo have the courage to demand a raise in status.

1961 AWARD   **Island of the Blue Dolphins.** Scott O'Dell. Houghton.

Accidentally left behind when her tribe flees, Karana spends eighteen years alone on an island off the coast of California. Her courage and resourcefulness help her to survive and to fill her life with moments of beauty and happiness.

Honors   **America Moves Forward: A History for Peter.**
Gerald W. Johnson. Illustrated by Leonard Everett Fisher. Morrow.
From World War I to 1956, major events and important men of politics are evaluated and discussed for their impact on American life and history. The third and final volume in a work that offers a personalized look at American history, the book is illustrated with striking scratchboard pictures.

Old Ramon. Jack Schaefer. Illustrated by Harold West. Houghton.
Old Ramon teaches the boy as much as he can during the months they spend with the sheep in the mountains. Along

the way, Ramon shares stories of his youth as a shepherd with the boy's grandfather and brings the boy back to the valley with a keener understanding and appreciation for the life of a shepherd.

The Cricket in Times Square. George Selden, pseud. (George Thompson). Illustrated by Garth Williams. Farrar.
Accidentally brought into a New York City subway station, Chester Cricket is found by Mario Bellini, the son of a newsstand owner. Chester is befriended by two subway animals, Harry Cat and Tucker Mouse, who encourage him to use his musical talents to help the Bellinis. An overnight success, Chester nonetheless longs to return to the country.

1960 AWARD

Onion John. Joseph Krumgold. Illustrated by Symeon Shimin. Crowell.

Twelve-year-old Andy is torn between his love for his father and his affection for Onion John, the old man whose way of life is totally foreign to nearly everyone in town. When members of the Rotary Club try to build Onion John a new house, their actions have great repercussions.

Honors

My Side of the Mountain. Jean Craighead George. Dutton.
Tired of living in a crowded city apartment, Sam Gribley runs away from home and heads for his Grandpa Gribley's long-lost homestead in the Catskill mountains. For a year he stays alone, learning to live off the land, hollowing out a tree for a home, taming a falcon, and using every bit of ingenuity and resourcefulness he has to survive.

America Is Born: A History for Peter. Gerald W. Johnson. Illustrated by Leonard Everett Fisher. Morrow.
Johnson's account of America's history is a very personal retelling of the lives and adventures of the people who explored and settled this country. The first in a three-volume series, the book covers the time from Columbus to the Revolutionary War and the Constitutional Convention.

The Gammage Cup. Carol Kendall. Illustrated by Erik Blegvad. Harcourt.
Five misfits are sent into exile in the mountains when they refuse to conform to Minnepin traditions of dress, ideas, and life-style. They come to the rescue of the Land Between the Mountains when they uncover an invasion plot by the Mushroom People.

1959 AWARD

The Witch of Blackbird Pond. Elizabeth George Speare. Houghton.

When her grandfather dies, sixteen-year-old Kit leaves the West Indies to live with her Puritan Aunt Rachel and her family. Kit's lively personality, her bright clothes, and her friendship with an outcast Quaker woman make her a target for charges of witchcraft in 1687 New England.

Honors

The Family under the Bridge. Natalie S. Carlson. Illustrated by Garth Williams. Harper.

Armand, who wanders the streets of Paris without a care, finds that his place beneath a bridge has been invaded by three children and their mother. Though he does not want to have anything to do with the children, the old man soon becomes a grandfather figure to the family, helping them, sharing the fun of the city, and ultimately making them his responsibility.

Along Came a Dog. Meindert DeJong. Illustrated by Maurice Sendak. Harper.

When her frostbitten toes fall off, the little red hen becomes a target for the other chickens' abuse. Only the big, homeless dog comes to her rescue, looking on her as something to guard and love as he tries to make the farm his home.

Chucaro: Wild Pony of the Pampa. Francis Kalnay. Illustrated by Julian de Miskey. Harcourt.

Once wild on the Argentine pampa, Chucaro is captured and tamed by Pedrito and his gaucho friend Juan. When the patron demands a gentle horse for his spoiled and cruel son, it is Chucaro he gets in spite of Pedrito's determination to keep him.

The Perilous Road. William O. Steele. Illustrated by Paul Galdone. Harcourt.

Eleven-year-old Chris passionately hates the Yankees invading his Tennessee homeland and wants to do anything to help the South. He is deaf to his father's words when he says war is the worst thing that can happen to people. Then Chris is caught in the middle of a savage battle and realizes how horrible war really is.

1958 AWARD

Rifles for Watie. Harold Keith. Crowell.

Sixteen-year-old Jeff, already a combat veteran in the Union Army and winner of the Congressional Medal of Honor, is captured by the rebel troops of General Stand Watie, a Cherokee Indian, and forced to become one of his scouts.

Honors

Gone-Away Lake. Elizabeth Enright. Illustrated by Beth and Joe Krush. Harcourt.

All summer Julian and his ten-year-old cousin Portia explore the houses they discover around Gone-Away Lake. They tell no one about the place or the two old people living in one of the houses until a near tragedy exposes their secret.

Tom Paine, Freedom's Apostle. Leo Gurko. Illustrated by Fritz Kredel. Crowell.

With hardly any education or money and only Ben Franklin's letter of introduction, Tom Paine goes to America and writes *Common Sense*, the first of his revolutionary pamphlets. The power and vision of Paine's writings and the violent feelings they aroused throughout his life are evident in this biography.

The Great Wheel. Robert Lawson. Viking.

Aunt Honoria predicts that Conn will leave Ireland and head west. Now he is in Chicago working on a construction project for a man named Ferris. His aunt has also made the wild prediction that he will ride the world's biggest wheel. Conn does as soon as Mr. Ferris's daring project is completed for the Chicago World's Columbian Exposition of 1893.

The Horsecatcher. Mari Sandoz. Westminster.

Unlike the other Cheyenne boys, Young Elk refuses to kill. He wants to capture and tame the wild horses of the prairie. When his father insists he join in their war, he runs away, returning months later with fifteen horses and the start of what becomes a nearly legendary way with wild horses.

1957 AWARD

Miracles on Maple Hill. Virginia Sorensen. Illustrated by Beth and Joe Krush. Harcourt.

When her father finally returns from being a prisoner of war, Marley's family decides to try to make a new beginning on a beautiful farm in Pennsylvania. During their first year there, they marvel at the miracle of the sap rising in the maple trees and the changes in each other.

Honors

Black Fox of Lorne. Marguerite de Angeli. Doubleday.

Shipwrecked off the coast of medieval Scotland, identical twins Jan and Brus are the only ones left alive when their father and his men are murdered. They survive by tricking the Scots into thinking that only one of them exists. Having sworn to avenge their father's murder, they foil the man's treasonous plot and keep their vow.

The House of Sixty Fathers. Meindert DeJong. Illustrated by Maurice Sendak. Harper.
Alone in his family sampan, Tien Pao lands in Japanese-occupied China and begins a dangerous journey back to Hengyang during World War II. On his way, a company of American airmen adopt him, and he finds himself with sixty strange but kind fathers who help him find his family.

Old Yeller. Fred Gipson. Illustrated by Carl Burger. Harper.
Left to help care for the homestead while his father takes their cattle to Kansas, fourteen-year-old Travis initially resents the intrusion of the big yellow dog. The dog proves his worth by rescuing little Arliss from a bear and Travis from wild hogs, guaranteeing himself a home.

Mr. Justice Holmes. Clara Ingram Judson. Illustrated by Robert Todd. Follett.
The son of a famous writer, Oliver Wendell Holmes, Jr. is a daydreamer whose brilliance is not always apparent to his family. After serving in the Civil War, he becomes a lawyer and a teacher, trying to make law interesting and clear to those entering the profession. Well-respected but never wealthy, he becomes one of the country's most highly esteemed Supreme Court justices.

The Corn Grows Ripe. Dorothy Rhoads. Illustrated by Jean Charlot. Viking.
A happy but often irresponsible twelve-year-old Yucatan boy must suddenly grow up when his father is injured. Tigre bravely goes to another village to get a bonesetter and then sets about clearing and burning the family's new corn field, a ritualized duty that goes back to Mayan times. He proves he can be reliable.

1956 AWARD

Carry On, Mr. Bowditch. Jean Lee Latham. Illustrated by John O'Hara Cosgrove. Houghton.

In spite of having little education, Nat Bowditch manages to teach himself mathematics and the principles of navigation. When he gets the chance to sail as a second mate, he teaches the rest of the crew to navigate and even finds mistakes in the navigational tables. He later rewrites the tables, and they become a standard navigational tool.

Honors

The Golden Name Day. Jennie Lindquist. Illustrated by Garth Williams. Harper.

Staying with her Swedish-American grandparents while her mother is hospitalized, Nancy is warmly welcomed into an extended family of aunts, uncles, and cousins. With everyone else having a special Swedish Name Day to celebrate, the family unsuccessfully tries to find a matching Swedish name for Nancy. Only when a new family moves in is Nancy's problem solved.

The Secret River. Marjorie Kinnan Rawlings. Illustrated by Leonard Weisgard. Scribner.
When hard times come to the Florida forest people, little Calpurnia and her dog, Buggyhorse, go to the wise woman of the forest for help. Advised to follow her nose, Calpurnia discovers a beautiful river full of fish. She catches many and brings them home, making hard times "soft."

Men, Microscopes, and Living Things. Katherine Shippen. Illustrated by Anthony Ravielli. Viking.
The author begins with Aristotle and his investigation of natural science, then moves on to Pliny, Harvey, Linnaeus, Lamarck, and others. The lively yet factual writing provides interesting insights into the work of significant biologists.

1955 AWARD

The Wheel on the School. Meindert DeJong. Illustrated by Maurice Sendak. Harper.

Inspired by Lina's composition about storks, her classmates and teacher decide to find a way to bring the birds and their luck back to their little Dutch village. As the children involve the people of the village in the search for a wheel and for a way to attach it to their school, they bring their small community together.

Honors

Courage of Sarah Noble. Alice Dalgliesh. Illustrated by Leonard Weisgard. Scribner.
"Keep up your courage," Sarah's mother tells her when she leaves with her father to build a home in the wilderness. The home finished, Sarah stays with friendly Indians while her father goes back for the rest of the family.

Banner in the Sky. James Ullman. Lippincott.
Although his father died trying to climb the Citadel, the highest mountain in the Alps, Rudy is determined to scale it himself. He hides his climbing ability from his mother and his Alpine-guide uncle and joins an English expedition hoping to be able to plant his father's red shirt at the top as a banner in the sky.

1954 AWARD

... And Now Miguel. Joseph Krumgold. Illustrated by Jean Charlot. Crowell.

Every spring Miguel hopes this is the year he will be asked to join the men as they take their sheep up into the Sangre de Cristo Mountains of New Mexico. When at the age of twelve he is told it is not yet time for him, he works hard and prays that his father will see how grown-up he is.

Honors

All Alone. Claire Huchet Bishop. Illustrated by Feodor Rojankovsky. Viking.

When his father sends him to the high pastures with the heifers, Marcel is forcefully reminded of the village motto, "Each man for himself." But loneliness makes the yodel of another boy welcome, and when disaster strikes, Marcel is saved by his willingness to help someone else.

Magic Maize. Mary and Conrad Buff. Illustrated by the authors. Houghton.

With the gringo world encroaching on the old ways of the Indians of Guatemala, a father continues to teach his son the old ways of farming and of praying to the gods of planting and harvest. Yet when their crop fails, it is the gringos who come to the family's aid.

Hurry Home, Candy. Meindert DeJong. Illustrated by Maurice Sendak. Harper.

Taken from his mother before he is weaned and given to a family that only knows how to hurt and control him, Candy is lost on a family outing and becomes a stray. He longs for his own home and for people who will really love him.

Shadrach. Meindert DeJong. Illustrated by Maurice Sendak. Harper.

After Davie's grandfather promises him a rabbit of his own, the little boy's excitement is nearly uncontainable. Davie bravely gathers food near a dangerous Dutch canal, helps get his hutch ready, and, when the rabbit arrives, lavishes attention and affection on the little animal.

Theodore Roosevelt, Fighting Patriot. Clara Ingram Judson. Illustrated by Lorence F. Bjorklund. Follett.

Independent and honorable, Theodore is forever facing challenges because of his poor health, bad vision, and determination to learn as much as he can. As an adult he is remembered for leading the Rough Riders up San Juan Hill, starting our national park system, and being a president with tremendous courage and integrity.

1953 AWARD

Secret of the Andes. Ann Nolan Clark. Illustrated by Jean Charlot. Viking.

Determined to discover another way of life, Cusi leaves his beautiful Incan home in the Andes Mountains and goes to the lowlands of Spanish Peru. Once there he longs for the hidden valley and the Old One. He returns knowing that he will never again willingly leave his home or break his vow to keep the Incan secret.

Honors

The Bears on Hemlock Mountain. Alice Dalgliesh. Illustrated by Helen Sewell. Scribner.

"There are no bears on Hemlock Mountain, no bears at all," Jonathan repeats as he goes over the mountain to borrow the big iron pot. But on the way back, Jonathan learns that there are indeed bears on Hemlock Mountain.

Birthdays of Freedom, Vol. I. Genevieve Foster. Scribner.

Starting with the excitement of the signing of the Declaration of Independence, the author sweeps back in time to the cave dwellers. From that time to the fall of Rome in 476 A.D., the determination to gain freedom is shown as the spark that encourages great inventions, discoveries, and political movements.

Moccasin Trail. Eloise Jarvis McGraw. Illustrated by Paul Galdone. Coward.

A runaway who is clawed by a grizzly and left for dead, Jim is raised by the Crow Indians and becomes a mountain man. Receiving a letter from his little brother asking for help, Jim finds his orphaned family on a wagon train heading to Oregon. He agrees to stay with them on the dangerous journey west. It is Jim's courage and Crow training that help them survive.

Red Sails to Capri. Ann Weil. Illustrated by C. B. Falls. Viking.

Three wealthy strangers come to Michele's small island village and stay at his parents' inn. Their good spirits and desire for adventure soon convince Michele and his friends to help the strangers explore a forbidden cave. Their discovery of the now-famous Blue Grotto changes the lives of everyone on Capri.

Charlotte's Web. E. B. White. Illustrated by Garth Williams. Harper.

After being raised by the farmer's daughter, Wilbur, a pig, is sold to another farm where his companion is a gray spider named Charlotte. When it becomes apparent that Wilbur is being fattened up for slaughtering, Charlotte promises to save him. The words that begin appearing in Charlotte's web amaze the farmer and bring hope to Wilbur.

1952 AWARD   **Ginger Pye.** Eleanor Estes. Harcourt.

The only clue to the mysterious disappearance of Ginger, the Pye family dog, is the unusual man in the mustard-colored hat. Jerry and Rachel look everywhere for their little dog, occasionally seeing the mustard-hatted man, and finally solve the mystery of Ginger's disappearance.

Honors   **Americans before Columbus.** Elizabeth Baity. Illustrated by C. B. Falls. Viking.

A study of pre-Columbian peoples in the Americas, this book describes their art, architecture, music, literature, and culture from the earliest times to that of Columbus. The text is prefaced with photographs of art and architecture and includes ink drawings in every chapter.

The Apple and the Arrow. Mary and Conrad Buff. Houghton.
Caught by tyrant Gessler's soldier, Walter's father, William Tell, is forced to either shoot an apple on Walter's head or die. He successfully shoots the apple but is imprisoned. Breaking free, Tell kills Gessler and starts the revolution that wins Switzerland's freedom.

Minn of the Mississippi. Holling C. Holling. Houghton.
Over a twenty-five-year period a snapping turtle makes her way from the source of the Mississippi to the Delta. Along the way she encounters a variety of adventures, lays eggs as she grows older, and introduces readers to the varied people, places, and wildlife along the river.

The Defender. Nicholas Kalashnikoff. Illustrated by Claire and George Louden. Scribner.
In turn-of-the-century Siberia, Turgen, a widowed hunter and herbalist, becomes the target of the local shaman when he begins to protect the shy, fast-disappearing mountain rams. Turgen's only friends are a poor widow, whom he befriends and marries, and her two children.

The Light at Tern Rock. Julia L. Sauer. Illustrated by Georges Schreiber. Viking.
Although Mr. Flagg has promised to get them back to shore by December 15, Aunt Martha and Ronnie suddenly realize that they are stuck at the lonely lighthouse until after Christmas. At first angry and sullen, Ronnie finally joins Aunt Martha in a very special celebration of the holiday.

1951 AWARD

Amos Fortune, Free Man. Elizabeth Yates. Illustrated by Nora S. Unwin. Dutton.

Captured by slavers, Amos, son of an African king, survives the long ocean voyage only to be sold to a New England Quaker. After years of serving and learning from others, Amos buys his own freedom, sets up his own business, and begins to buy and set free other slaves.

Honors

Gandhi, Fighter without a Sword. Jeanette Eaton. Illustrated by Ralph Ray. Morrow.

From an upper-class life in India, Gandhi travels to England where he becomes a lawyer. Later he goes to South Africa and becomes involved in fighting for civil liberties. Back in India, Gandhi spends the remainder of his life leading the nonviolent independence movement, which finally brings freedom to India and martyrdom to Gandhi.

Better Known as Johnny Appleseed. Mabel Leigh Hunt. Illustrated by James Daugherty. Lippincott.

Loved by the settlers and the Indians, John Chapman carves a new name and legend for himself by trekking through the wilderness planting apple trees and helping anyone in need. The few facts known about Chapman are carefully interwoven with the Johnny Appleseed legends.

Abraham Lincoln, Friend of the People. Clara Ingram Judson. Illustrated with drawings by Robert Frankenberg and Kodachromes of the Chicago Historical Society Lincoln Dioramas. Follett.

Vividly written and carefully researched, the book portrays the struggles Abraham Lincoln has in learning to read, making a living, and finally entering politics. The difficulties of life on the frontier and the problems leading to the Civil War form the background.

The Story of Appleby Capple. Anne Parrish. Harper.

For his Cousin Clement's ninety-ninth birthday, five-year-old Appleby is determined to give the old man the thing he wants most to see: a zebra butterfly. The boy wanders through the alphabet looking for the butterfly. Ink illustrations work people and objects around all twenty-six letters.

1950 AWARD

The Door in the Wall. Marguerite de Angeli. Doubleday.

Crippled by a strange disease, Robin is ready to give up since he knows he will never be a knight. Then the monks help him to find ways to gain strength and courage and ultimately to play an important role in saving his medieval city.

Honors

Tree of Freedom. Rebecca Caudill. Illustrated by
Dorothy B. Morse. Viking.

During the American Revolution, the Venable family leaves
North Carolina to seek new land and get away from British
oppression. Their exciting month-long trek over the
mountains to Kentucky starts them on the way to new
freedom, symbolized by the apple tree, whose seeds have
come with the family all the way from France.

The Blue Cat of Castle Town. Catherine Coblentz. Illustrated by Janice Holland. Longmans.

Born under a blue moon, the little kitten is destined to carry
the river's song of beauty, peace, and contentment to the
unhappy people of Castle Town, Vermont. They have
exchanged beauty for money, no longer making things with
honesty and unable to "sing their own songs."

George Washington. Genevieve Foster. Scribner.

Filled with interesting excerpts from letters and diaries, this
animated portrayal of the first president of the United States
tells of George Washington's childhood and his many
challenges as surveyor, soldier, commander in chief, and
president.

**Song of the Pines: A Story of Norwegian Lumbering in
Wisconsin.** Walter and Marion Havighurst. Illustrated
by Richard Floethe. Winston.

An orphan, fifteen-year-old Nils joins the Svendsen family
and other Norwegian emigrants as they head toward
America in the 1850s. They travel to Wisconsin where they
stake out a claim for a farm. Nils, having found work in the
lumber camps, creates his own business and future in
America.

Kildee House. Rutherford Montgomery. Illustrated by
Barbara Cooney. Doubleday.

Not used to talking or being around people, Jerome Kildee
retires to a small house he builds atop a hill in the redwood
forest of northern California. Through the animals he
shelters and the young people he meets, Kildee's life and the
lives of those he encounters become fuller and richer than he
ever imagined.

1949 AWARD

King of the Wind. Marguerite Henry. Illustrated by
Wesley Dennis. Rand McNally.

Sure that the motherless Arabian colt is going to be a great
racer, Agba, the Sultan's mute slaveboy, raises the animal

and stays with it, even when the horse is sent to France. Times are hard for the two, and they are often treated cruelly, but Agba never gives up his belief in the horse that becomes the ancestor of the great Man o' War.

Honors   **Story of the Negro.** Arna Bontemps. Illustrated by Raymond Lufkin. Knopf.

Beginning with the first slave ship to come to Jamestown, Bontemps celebrates the culture and accomplishments of black people throughout the world: from the cultural heritage of Africa to the artists, leaders, and momentous events that have shaped not only black but world culture as well.

My Father's Dragon. Ruth S. Gannett. Illustrated by Ruth Chrisman Gannett. Random House.

An old alley cat convinces the narrator's father to rescue a baby dragon being used as a ferry by the animals of faraway Wild Island. With chewing gum, toothpaste, lollipops, and ribbons, the little boy keeps lions and tigers from eating him as he tries to rescue the little dragon.

Seabird. Holling C. Holling. Houghton.

To help him while away the hours on the whaling ship, Ezra carves a mascot, Seabird, which becomes his constant companion as he journeys around the world and finally gets his own ship. For four generations Seabird brings companionship and luck to Ezra's family as they sail the sea.

Daughter of the Mountain. Louise Rankin. Illustrated by Kurt Wiese. Viking.

When Momo's beloved Lhasa terrier is stolen by a wool trader, the Tibetan girl follows him on a long and dangerous journey that takes her through the mountains into India and finally to Calcutta.

1948 AWARD   **The Twenty-One Balloons.** William Pène du Bois. Viking.

Professor Sherman leaves San Francisco in one hot air balloon and three weeks later is found in the Atlantic Ocean, clinging to the remains of twenty balloons and refusing to tell how he got there.

Honors   **The Quaint and Curious Quest of Johnny Longfoot.** Catherine Besterman. Illustrated by Warren Chappell. Bobbs-Merrill.

Sent to the country to stay with his very thrifty uncle, Johnny, son of the shoe king, outwits guard dogs and a bear to reach the miserly old man. Not welcome, he goes on a quest that leads him to a cat who sends him to look for gold and seven-league boots. Leading a band of dogs, cats, bears, and his tagalong uncle, Johnny resourcefully succeeds in his mission.

Pancakes-Paris. Claire Huchet Bishop. Illustrated by Georges Schreiber. Viking.

Before the war there was heat and food and paper. Now Charles wishes for a way to show his little sister the fun of Mardi Gras and the wonderful crepes they ate. When two American soldiers suddenly enter his life and give him a strange box that they claim holds the ingredients for crepes, things start to happen.

The Cow-tail Switch, and Other West African Stories. Harold Courlander. Illustrated by Madye Lee Chastain. Holt.

Puns, trickster tales, creation tales, parables, and proverbs form the basis for these seventeen stories from West Africa. Faithfully retold from original sources, the stories are great fun to read or tell.

Li Lun, Lad of Courage. Carolyn Treffinger. Illustrated by Kurt Wiese. Abingdon.

When Li Lun refuses to join his father on his trip out to sea, the man angrily sends the boy up to the top of their mountain to grow rice. Alone on the mountaintop for 120 days, Li Lun, called a coward by his father and the other boys, courageously faces the elements, determined to complete his task.

Misty of Chincoteague. Marguerite Henry. Illustrated by Wesley Dennis. Rand McNally.

When Pony Penning Day comes on Chincoteague Island, Maureen and Paul are determined to buy the Phantom and her filly, Misty. They work hard and save $102, and finally the two spirited animals are theirs. Now the children must train the wild ponies to be around people, instead of running wild on Assateague.

1947 AWARD

Miss Hickory. Carolyn Sherwin Bailey. Illustrated by Ruth Gannett. Viking.

With an apple twig for a body and a hickory nut for a head, Miss Hickory stubbornly refuses help as she tries to survive a cold New Hampshire winter alone.

Honors

Wonderful Year. Nancy Barnes. Illustrated by Kate Seredy. Messner.

Eleven-year-old Ellen and her fun-loving parents move from an easy life in Kansas to a ranch in western Colorado. They enjoy life as they plant trees and build a home and a barn. For Ellen, the best part is her friendship with fifteen-year-old Ronnie and the adventures they share.

Big Tree. Mary and Conrad Buff. Viking.

A glorious tree that can live thousands of years and has no fear of fire or insects, the redwood Wawona begins to grow long before the pyramids and the coming of Christ. Nothing threatens the huge and ancient tree until man arrives with axes and saws. But others recognize his importance and offer protection to the redwood.

The Avion My Uncle Flew. Cyrus Fisher, pseud. (Darwin L. Teilhet). Illustrated by Richard Floethe. Appleton.

When John's father returns home after World War II, he decides to take his wife and son to France. There John will have a chance to get his injured leg treated and to see his mother's homeland. John does not want to go, but he has no choice. Once there he becomes involved in a mysterious adventure that takes him to southern France and his glider-building uncle.

The Heavenly Tenants. William Maxwell. Illustrated by Ilonka Karasz. Harper.

The night before the Maxwells are to leave for three weeks in Virginia, father takes the children outside and shows them the different constellations that make up the zodiac. When no one comes to care for their animals while they are gone, the signs of the zodiac come to Earth and do it for them.

The Hidden Treasure of Glaston. Eleanore Jewett. Illustrated by Frederick T. Chapman. Viking.

When he is forced to leave the country because of his part in the murder of Thomas à Becket, Sir Hugh de Morville leaves his crippled son in the care of the monks at Glaston. As the boy and a new friend explore the area, they discover treasure left by King Arthur and his court and begin an exciting and suspenseful search for the Holy Grail.

1946 AWARD   **Strawberry Girl.** Lois Lenski. Lippincott.

Birdie's family wants to make a good living growing strawberries and oranges in turn-of-the-century Florida. Unfortunately their shiftless neighbors, the Slaters, fight them every step of the way.

Honors   **Justin Morgan Had a Horse.** Marguerite Henry. Illustrated by Wesley Dennis. Rand McNally.

Justin Morgan does not want the little colt that follows him and Joel home. But Joel raises and trains it, and the two soon realize that the little horse is something very special, not to mention very fast. Years later it becomes the first of a new breed: the Justin Morgan horse.

The Moved-Outers. Florence Crannell Means. Illustrated by Helen Blair. Houghton.

After the attack on Pearl Harbor, the Ohara family, who have always thought of themselves as Americans, are suddenly "Japanese." Put into internment camps with only the barest of necessities, Sue and her family try not only to survive but to stay loyal Americans.

New Found World. Katherine Shippen. Illustrated by C. B. Falls. Viking.

A history of Latin America, the book begins with a chapter on the topography and the plant and animal life of the area. Additional chapters discuss the native peoples and their interaction with European explorers and colonists. Well-researched, the book covers aspects of Latin American life and history up to the end of World War II.

Bhimsa, the Dancing Bear. Christine Weston. Illustrated by Roger Duvioisin. Scribner.

While aimlessly walking in his Indian garden, David is surprised by the approach of a boy, Gopala, and his tame bear, Bhimsa. He eagerly runs away with the two as they wander through India trying to find a way home for Gopala. Bhimsa's dancing attracts attention everywhere, earning them food and getting them into and out of trouble along the way.

1945 AWARD **Rabbit Hill.** Robert Lawson. Viking.

The excitement among the wild creatures is contagious as Little Georgie enthusiastically tells every one of them that new folks are coming to the old farmhouse. All of the animals anxiously await the day the newcomers will arrive, afraid they might be the kind who have guns or dogs or even poison.

Honors **The Silver Pencil.** Alice Dalgliesh. Illustrated by Katherine Milhous. Scribner.

After her father's sudden death, Janet and her mother begin a series of moves that take them from Trinidad, to England, to the United States, and then to Nova Scotia. Along the way, Janet holds fast to the silver pencil her father gave her, finding that writing is a solace.

Lone Journey: The Life of Roger Williams. Jeanette Eaton. Illustrated by Woodi Ishmael. Harcourt.
From childhood onward, Roger Williams is a champion for religious freedom. Again and again he speaks out for separation of church and state, risking his own life and trying to save the lives of others. Finally Williams becomes the founder of the Providence Colony in America, where settlers of all religious faiths can find refuge.

The Hundred Dresses. Eleanor Estes. Illustrated by Louis Slobodkin. Harcourt.
Wanda Petronski, who speaks in broken English and always wears the same sparkling clean dress to school each day, brags to the other girls that she has a hundred dresses at home. Wanda is laughed at and teased by the other girls, and she and her family move away. Only then do the girls find Wanda's beautifully drawn pictures of one hundred dresses.

Abraham Lincoln's World. Genevieve Foster. Scribner.
As Abraham Lincoln grows from birth to death, the things happening throughout the world affect him and his country. Chapter by chapter the stories of not only Lincoln but also Napolean, Jefferson, Tecumseh, Jackson, Bismarck, and others are told alternately to give a full and fascinating picture of world events.

1944 AWARD

Johnny Tremain. Esther Forbes. Illustrated by Lynd Ward. Houghton.

Fourteen-year-old apprentice silversmith Johnny Tremain has a terrible accident that forces him to give up his work. He becomes involved with Sam Adams and the other Boston patriots, takes part in the Boston Tea Party, and plays a role in the Battle of Lexington.

Honors

Rufus M. Eleanor Estes. Illustrated by Louis Slobodkin. Harcourt.
A lively and imaginative little boy, Rufus is the youngest of the four Moffat children. Anxious to do his part for the war effort, he knits washcloths, plants a victory garden, and earns enough money selling popcorn to become a Victory Boy.

Fog Magic. Julia Sauer. Illustrated by Lynd Ward. Viking.
In every generation of Addingtons there is one person for whom the dense fog of Nova Scotia is magical. Walking toward the deserted village of Blue Cove on a foggy day, Greta comes upon a thriving village she has never seen before. It is the Blue Cove of one hundred years ago.

These Happy Golden Years. Laura Ingalls Wilder. Illustrated by Helen Sewell and Mildred Boyle. Harper.
Laura Ingalls, though still a student herself, begins teaching in small schools and sewing to earn tuition money for Mary's education. Whether working hard in town, teaching, living on her family's claim on the Dakota prairie, or finally deciding to marry Almanzo, Laura realizes how lucky she is to have her warm, happy family.

Mountain Born. Elizabeth Yates. Illustrated by Nora S. Unwin. Coward.
Nursed back to life by Peter's mother, Biddy, a black lamb, is given to six-year-old Peter to raise. Bright and brave, Biddy becomes the leader of the herd, repeatedly alerting her human keepers to impending disaster.

1943 AWARD

Adam of the Road. Elizabeth Janet Gray. Illustrated by Robert Lawson. Viking.

Adam, his minstrel father, their horse, and Adam's trained dog, Nick, are traveling in thirteenth-century England, singing and telling stories for food and a place to sleep. When Nick is stolen, father and son try desperately to find him and become separated from each other.

Honors

The Middle Moffat. Eleanor Estes. Illustrated by Louis Slobodkin. Harcourt.
Janey is the "middle Moffat," trying hard to be serious and to do everything well. Things do not seem to work out quite as she plans (her organ recital turns into an escape for thousands of moths), but the little girl is undeterred. She continues to make bold plans with outrageously funny results.

"Have You Seen Tom Thumb?" Mabel Leigh Hunt. Illustrated by Fritz Eichenberg. Lippincott.
From the age of five, Charles Sherwood Stratton, only twenty-five inches tall and weighing fifteen pounds, is presented to the world by P. T. Barnum as General Tom Thumb. A charming, humorous person, he travels all over the world with Barnum.

1942 AWARD

The Matchlock Gun. Walter Edmonds. Illustrated by Paul Lantz. Dodd.

Edward, his mother, and his little sister have only one defense against the French and the Indians — a huge matchlock gun. When attacked, his mother is wounded, and Edward must use the gun to save their lives.

Honors **George Washington's World.** Genevieve Foster. Scribner.
From birth to death, the story of George Washington's life and the lives of other well-known kings, soldiers, politicians, and scientists of the same period are interwoven. In each section the author skillfully provides a worldview of events.

Down Ryton Water. Eva Roe Gaggin. Illustrated by Elmer Hader. Viking.
Escaping the religious persecution of their English countrymen, Matt and his family and neighbors head down Ryton Water for freedom in Holland. Finally ready to face the long and dangerous voyage to the New World, all of them board the *Mayflower* and *Speedwell* to sail to what becomes the Plymouth Colony.

Indian Captive: The Story of Mary Jemison. Lois Lenski. Lippincott.
Even though other settlers have been slaughtered by the French and the Indians, Pa refuses to let his family go east to safety. They, too, are captured, and only young, blond-haired Mary survives, forced to become a part of the Seneca people.

Little Town on the Prairie. Laura Ingalls Wilder. Illustrated by Helen Sewell and Mildred Boyle. Harper.
Laura is fifteen and, in warm weather, working hard with Ma and Pa on their Dakota Territory claim. She earns what she can to help pay for Mary's courses at the College for the Blind, and, with her family, she spends the long, cold, but friend-filled winters in town.

1941 AWARD **Call It Courage.** Armstrong Sperry. Macmillan.
Mocked by the other boys because of his fear of the sea, Mafatu secretly takes a small boat and leaves his village. Alone on a terrifying ocean voyage, the boy, son of a Polynesian chief, overcomes his fear of the sea.

Honors **Young Mac of Fort Vancouver.** Mary Jane Carr. Illustrated by Richard Holberg. Crowell.
Traveling west to Fort Vancouver in 1832, Young Mac is determined to become a fur-trading Northman and not a full-fledged member of the white world. Contact with Dr. McLoughlan, head of the fort, and other white and mixed-heritage men causes him to reconsider his decision.

Blue Willow. Doris Gates. Illustrated by Paul Lantz. Viking.

With her small family wandering from place to place so that Dad can find work, Janey has never really had a home or school or friends. Maybe the San Joaquin Valley will be the place where everything changes, a place where they can stay and she can finally bring the blue willow plate out for good.

Nansen. Anna Gertrude Hall. Illustrated by Boris Artzybasheff. Viking.

Determined to learn as much as he can as a little boy (and even more determined as an adult), Fridtjof Nansen grows to be one of Norway's most famous citizens. He is an explorer who travels all the way to the North Pole, a statesman, and, most difficult of all, a fighter for world peace and a winner of the Nobel Peace Prize.

The Long Winter. Laura Ingalls Wilder. Illustrated by Helen Sewell and Mildred Boyle. Harper.

The Ingalls family, pioneering in the Dakota Territory, stoically endure a dreary succession of blizzards. Huddled in the family store, they and their neighbors must depend upon their ingenuity to prevent freezing and starvation.

1940 AWARD

Daniel Boone. James Daugherty. Viking.

A rugged frontiersman and a leader of pioneers, Daniel Boone starts life in Pennsylvania and ends it eighty-six years later in Missouri, an almost legendary character. Boone's longing for adventure, his bravery, and his foolishness are examined honestly in this biography that sings the praises of pioneer men and women in words and vigorous drawings.

Honors

Boy with a Pack. Stephen W. Meader. Illustrated by Edward Shenton. Harcourt.

Bill fills a backpack with things to sell in Ohio and, with two years of savings, leaves his New Hampshire mill town on foot. The 1837 journey is long and hard but filled with all kinds of adventures, danger, and amazing good luck.

Runner of the Mountain Tops: The Life of Louis Agassiz. Mabel Robinson. Illustrated by Lynd Ward. Random House.

A brilliant naturalist and the founder of Harvard's Agassiz Museum, Louis Agassiz is realistically portrayed from his childhood in Switzerland through his years as a Harvard professor. Agassiz's fascination with all of nature and his great teaching ability are evident throughout the book.

The Singing Tree. Kate Seredy. Viking.
Four years after the end of *The Good Master*, the First World
War has started, and Mother, Jancsi, and cousin Kate are left
to take care of the farm as Father and Uncle Sandor are
called to fight. The three of them hold the farm together and
make it a refuge for orphans, relatives, and even prisoners of
war.

By the Shores of Silver Lake. Laura Ingalls Wilder.
Illustrated by Helen Sewell and Mildred Boyle. Harper.
The Ingalls have not had a good crop since the grasshoppers
came. Pa decides they will make one more move, this time
to Dakota Territory. The family spends a happy winter
taking in other settlers and earning money to send Mary,
blind from scarlet fever, to a special school.

1939 AWARD

Thimble Summer. Elizabeth Enright. Farrar &
Rinehart.
All kinds of good things seem to happen after Garnet finds
the silver thimble in the dried-up river bed. The nine-year-
old farm girl notices that the drought finally breaks, she has
an exciting time being locked in the public library with a
friend, and her pet pig wins a blue ribbon at the fair.

Honors

Nino. Valenti Angelo. Viking.
While his father works in America to earn their fare to
California, Nino and his mother stay with his grandfather in
his small Italian village. The little boy and his family and
friends share holidays, trips to the city, and small but
exciting adventures that create a memorable picture of turn-
of-the-century Italy.

Mr. Popper's Penguins. Richard and Florence Atwater.
Illustrated by Robert Lawson. Little, Brown.
From the moment he is given a penguin as a pet, Mr.
Popper's life starts changing. He converts his basement into
an ice rink, finds a friend for his lonely bird, and suddenly
has twelve penguins to feed instead of one.

"Hello the Boat!" Phyllis Crawford. Illustrated by Edward
Laning. Holt.
The entire Doak family pitches in to get their store-boat from
Pittsburgh to Cincinnati in 1817. Along the Ohio River,
settlers shout out, "Hello the boat!" and the family eagerly
pushes the boat ashore and enthusiastically opens the store.
On their way, the Doaks encounter thieves, learn about the
history of the river area, and have a surprisingly good time.

Leader by Destiny: George Washington, Man and Patriot.
Jeanette Eaton. Illustrated by Jack Manley Rose. Harcourt.
Not a man who plans what he wants but rather one who
allows things to shape him and his future, George Washington lives a life full of adventure and responsibility as he
grows up. The fifty-two years of his life that Eaton covers
contain much of the history and many of the famous people
of his time.

Penn. Elizabeth Janet Gray. Illustrated by George Gillett
Whitney. Viking.
Until he converts to the Quaker religion, William Penn leads
a privileged upper-class life. Then he loses everything and is
imprisoned. After fighting hard for religious freedom, Penn
is allowed to go to America and found the new colony of
Pennsylvania, based on the principles for which he fought.

1938 AWARD

The White Stag. Kate Seredy. Viking.
Based on legends about the founding of Hungary, this
stirring story begins with Nimrod receiving a prophesy from
God. He tells his people to follow the White Stag and
Nimrod's sons to the west. During their long and dangerous
journey, the people move valiantly westward until the birth
of Attila, who one day leads them heroically into what
becomes Hungary.

Honors

Pecos Bill. James Cloyd Bowman. Illustrated by Laura
Bannon. Little, Brown.
Raised by coyotes and able to speak to animals, Pecos Bill
reluctantly accepts the knowledge that he is one of those
dreaded inhuman humans. He becomes a cowboy and does
things in legendary proportion: busting up a cyclone,
breaking up a cattle rustling gang, and rounding up
39,000,000 cattle and driving them to market.

Bright Island. Mabel Robinson. Illustrated by Lynd Ward.
Random House.
Strong, independent, and committed to life on her family's
small island off the coast of Maine, Thankful very reluctantly
agrees to attend school on the mainland. There, life is so
foreign that she initially feels like a total outsider among the
other high school students.

On the Banks of Plum Creek. Laura Ingalls Wilder.
Illustrated by Helen Sewell and Mildred Boyle. Harper.
After finally reaching Minnesota and planting a wheat crop,
the Ingalls lose it to a horde of grasshoppers. Determined to

stay, Pa goes to work for other farmers. Laura goes to school, shares adventures with friends, but most of all enjoys the moments when her family is together and Pa is back playing the fiddle.

1937 AWARD **Roller Skates.** Ruth Sawyer. Illustrated by Valenti Angelo. Viking.

Her wealthy parents in Europe, Lucinda spends a glorious year living with two teachers, skating all over New York City, and making friends everywhere. The people she meets, whether it is her impoverished musician neighbor or the hansom cab driver, appreciate her energy, friendliness, and determination.

Honors **The Golden Basket.** Ludwig Bemelmans. Viking.

A staid English father and his two little daughters visit Bruges, Belgium, and stay at the Golden Basket Hotel. The girls and the hotel owner's son enjoy exploring the famous city. While visiting a cathedral, they meet twelve little girls standing in two straight lines, the youngest and spunkiest being Madeline.

Winterbound. Margery Bianco. Viking.

With both of their parents gone for months, nineteen-year-old Kay and sixteen-year-old Garry take on managing both the rented cottage and their younger brother and sister. During a long, cold, but very exciting depression-era winter, they make friends, earn and save money, and gain strength and independence.

The Codfish Musket. Agnes Hewes. Illustrated by Armstrong Sperry. Doubleday.

Even as a youngster, Dan has a keen eye for fine rifles and arms. On a mission to Washington for his Boston employer, Dan becomes secretary to Thomas Jefferson. The president sends him into the frontier with a message for Merriwether Lewis, but along the way Dan spots gun thieves arming the Indians. He defeats them and delivers his message, finally returning to Washington.

Whistler's Van. Idwal Jones. Illustrated by Zhenya Gay. Viking.

After his grandfather disappears one night with a cart and pony, Gwilyn decides he wants a chance to wander through Wales as well. When the Ringos, a family of gypsies, appear at the farmhouse and whistle, Gwilyn goes off with them for a summer full of music, adventure, and, most importantly, horses.

Phebe Fairchild: Her Book. Lois Lenski. Stokes.
When Phebe's mother decides to join Phebe's father on a sea voyage, the ten-year-old is sent to stay with relatives in the country. Life in 1830 rural Connecticut at first seems rigid to Phebe, and her copy of Mother Goose is a constant source of support. The child comes to appreciate her relatives, their simple life, their generosity, and their sense of fun.

Audubon. Constance Rourke. Illustrated by James MacDonald. Harcourt.
Despite mysterious beginnings, John James Audubon manages to leave France and go to America. He marries but continues to traipse the countryside in search of birds and small animals to paint. Carefully researched, the book offers a well-rounded look at the man who became known for his nineteenth-century paintings of American birds.

1936 AWARD **Caddie Woodlawn.** Carol Ryrie Brink. Macmillan.

Eleven years old in 1864, Caddie roams the woods and rivers of western Wisconsin with her brothers as her mother relentlessly tries to make her into a young "lady." The mischievous redhead's adventures with Indians and pioneers are full of fun and excitement.

Honors **Young Walter Scott.** Elizabeth Janet Gray. Viking.
Despite years of living with country relatives, Walter is determined not to let his lame leg stand in his way once he is at home again. This lively, fictionalized biography transports readers to late eighteenth-century Edinburgh, Scotland, and offers an engrossing introduction to the life of the famous novelist.

The Good Master. Kate Seredy. Viking.
Jancsi is fascinated by his city cousin Kate's daring and reckless behavior. Whether she is stopping a stampede of horses, nearly drowning in the river, or running off with gypsies, she is a marvel and a delight to the Hungarian country folk.

All Sail Set: A Romance of the *Flying Cloud*. Armstrong Sperry. Winston.
Fifteen-year-old Thach goes to work for the great Donald McKay making drawings of his plans for the clipper ship *Flying Cloud*. The ship completed, Thach becomes an apprentice, sails around the Horn, is initiated by "Neptune," contends with mutineers, and nearly loses his life in a shipboard fire.

Honk, the Moose. Phil Stong. Illustrated by Kurt Wiese. Dodd. The temperature is thirty below zero and the snow is seven feet deep when the boys find a moose in Ivar's father's stable. The town is in an uproar as everyone tries to think of ways to get the gentle and very funny beast to leave.

1935 AWARD   **Dobry.** Monica Shannon. Illustrated by Atanas Katchamakoff. Viking.

Bulgarian peasant boy Dobry tries to convince his mother that he must be an artist. He does not want to plow the fields as his ancestors did. Dobry's grandfather understands, but until Dobry sculpts a beautiful nativity scene in the snow to prove his talents, his mother is not convinced.

Honors   **Davy Crockett.** Constance Rourke. Illustrated by James MacDonald. Harcourt.
Davy Crockett is a bigger-than-life character: he is a pioneer, hunter, teller of tales, soldier, statesman, and legendary American hero. Rourke writes a well-researched and well-documented biography filled with anecdotes and comments by Crockett and his contemporaries.

Pageant of Chinese History. Elizabeth Seeger. Illustrated by Bernard Watkins. Longmans.
Using a conversational style, Seeger leads the reader through Chinese history starting with mythical and legendary times. Then she writes about each of the dynasties, ending with the Manchu in 1912 and the beginning of the republic. Political and cultural history are the focus of most of the book.

A Day on Skates: The Story of a Dutch Picnic. Hilda Van Stockum. Harper.
The canals of Holland are finally frozen solid, and the headmaster has a surprise. He takes the children on an all-day skating picnic. In spite of a few accidents, it is a thoroughly enjoyable time. Many black-and-white drawings and eight full-color illustrations show the festive atmosphere of the day.

1934 AWARD   **Invincible Louisa: The Story of the Author of *Little Women*.** Cornelia Meigs. Little, Brown.

The life of Louisa May Alcott is chronicled through her lively involvement with family and friends. Incidents reveal that her invincible spirit keeps the family afloat during the darkest of times and always keeps them happy. Family photographs and a chronology are included.

The Winged Girl of Knossos. Erick Berry, pseud. (Allena Best). Appleton.
Spirited, athletic, and beautiful Inas, daughter of Daidalos, helps her father with his flying experiments on the Isle of Crete during the time of King Minos. Having to leave Crete hurriedly, she does so by flying out on a glider built by her father.

The Big Tree of Bunlahy: Stories of My Own Countryside. Padraic Colum. Illustrated by Jack Yeats. Macmillan.
Twelve fine old Irish tales and one original one are woven together by the storyteller who introduces each story. All are said to have been heard under the Tree of Bunlahy, the great elm tree with big, smooth stones under it. There the villagers would sit and listen to these tales of animals, heroes, and leprechans.

The ABC Bunny. Wanda Gäg. Coward.
Lithographs filled with curved lines show a bunny romping through his day. After being scared out of his bed by a crashing apple, the bunny meets many animals. Each large, bright red letter of the alphabet is accompanied by a text that carries the ABC lesson along in a rhythmic manner. The song, with words and music, is included.

Glory of the Seas. Agnes Hewes. Illustrated by N. C. Wyeth. Knopf.
The exciting early days of the clipper ships, the controversial Fugitive Slave Law, and the inner conflict caused by civil disobedience are at the center of this story set in Boston in the 1850s. When the *Flying Cloud* sails to San Francisco in just eighty-nine days, many Bostonians dream of sailing to California.

The Apprentice of Florence. Anne Kyle. Illustrated by Erick Berry, pseud. (Allena Best). Houghton.
Nemo, a sixteen-year-old Florentine apprentice, is sent to Constantinople on business in 1453. The city is besieged by Turks, and Nemo is hurt. On his return, young Christopher Columbus tells him that his father, thought to be dead, is alive. More adventures ensue as Nemo searches for his lost father.

New Land. Sarah Schmidt. Illustrated by Frank Dobias. McBride.
It is the 1930s when Dad, the seventeen-year-old twins, and their younger sister arrive in Wyoming to homestead on an unproved claim. Rivalries on the football field and in the new vocational school, a blinding snowstorm, and troubles

with the "big man" are overcome, and a new home is established.

Swords of Steel. Elsie Singmaster. Illustrated by David Hendrickson. Houghton.
Although he has heard talk of the differences between the North and the South, it is not until 1859, when his beloved, free black friend is kidnapped to be sold, that John feels personal involvement in the conflict. In six years John grows from childhood to manhood with the Civil War intruding on and then enveloping his life.

The Forgotten Daughter. Caroline Snedeker. Illustrated by Dorothy P. Lathrop. Doubleday.
When his wife dies in childbirth while he is traveling, the Roman centurion is told that both mother and child are dead. His daughter is subjected to the hardships of second-century life as a slave. Eventually she falls in love with a high-born Roman, and the plague unites her with her father.

1933 AWARD

Young Fu of the Upper Yangtze. Elizabeth Lewis. Illustrated by Kurt Wiese. Winston.

The empress has died and political life is in turmoil when Young Fu and his mother move from their village to Chungking so that he can be apprenticed to a coppersmith. Young Fu must constantly use his wits to protect his mother and himself from thieves and rascals.

Honors

Children of the Soil: A Story of Scandinavia. Nora Burglon. Illustrated by Edgar Parin d'Aulaire. Doubleday.
Two very poor but ambitious and industrious children live with their mother in Sweden at the turn of the twentieth century. The soil they hoe is poor, their crab trap washes out to sea, and a weaving contest is lost to the gentry. With a little help from a Tomte and a lot of work on their part, they acquire some livestock and the promise of a happier future.

Swift Rivers. Cornelia Meigs. Illustrated by Forrest W. Orr. Little, Brown.
When his mean-spirited uncle locks him out of the house where he was raised, Chris knows it is time to become a man. The harsh 1835 Wisconsin winter and the bountiful woods lead him to try floating logs down to St. Louis. As a part of the early days of the logging industry, Chris has many adventures on the river.

The Railroad to Freedom: A Story of the Civil War. Hildegarde Swift. Illustrated by James Daugherty. Harcourt.
Harriet Tubman, a slave, escapes from the South but goes back again and again, leading three hundred other slaves North to freedom via the dangerous Underground Railroad. The horrifying yet often thrilling adventures are based on incidents from Tubman's life.

1932 AWARD

Waterless Mountain. Laura Adams Armer. Illustrated by Sidney and Laura Armer. Longmans.

Destined to become a medicine man, introspective Younger Brother learns the songs and stories of the Navajo Indians and begins to create songs of his own. Skillfully interwoven into the story are the early twentieth-century culture and heritage of the tribe.

Honors

Jane's Island. Marjorie Allee. Illustrated by Maitland de Gorgoza. Houghton.
Ellen, a college freshman, spends the summer with twelve-year-old Jane in Woods Hole, Massachusetts, where Jane's father is a marine biologist. The girls enjoy light summer adventures while fishing and picnicking. Jane is a competent naturalist who imparts a good measure of scientific information throughout the story.

Truce of the Wolf and Other Tales of Old Italy. Mary Gould Davis. Illustrated by Jay Van Everen. Harcourt.
Seven widely varied Italian stories tell of such things as Saint Francis taming a menacing wolf, of an obstinate and heroic donkey, and of how a street in Florence was named. The tales, all told with a bit of Italian folk humor, come from many sources, including a Tuscan peasant woman and The Decameron.

Calico Bush. Rachel Field. Illustrated by Allen Lewis. Macmillan.
In 1743, twelve-year-old Marguerite is bound out to a family in Maine. Discriminated against by the parents because she is French, she finds happiness with the children as they all face hardships and the rigors of life in the Maine wilderness.

The Fairy Circus. Dorothy P. Lathrop. Macmillan.
When the circus tent goes up, it is so big that it encloses the places where the fairies live. They all scramble for the best view, and when it is over they decide to have a circus of their own. The fairies and woodland animals use grand imaginations as they re-create the circus in their own way.

Out of the Flame. Eloise Lownsbery. Illustrated by Elizabeth Tyler Wolcott. Longmans.

In the sixteenth century, Pierre is first a page then a squire as he becomes trained to be a knight in the court of Francis I. He attends tournaments, visits with great intellectuals, and learns music and botany with the royal children. Before the story ends, he and the children are abducted and released by pirates.

Boy of the South Seas. Eunice Tietjens. Illustrated by Myrtle Sheldon. Coward-McCann.
When a ship arrives in the harbor of the Marquesas Islands, young Teiki's curiosity gets ahold of him, and he climbs aboard and falls asleep. He awakens when the vessel is under sail and there is no turning back. At the island of Moorea, he swims ashore and makes a new life for himself.

1931 AWARD

The Cat Who Went to Heaven. Elizabeth Coatsworth. Illustrated by Lynd Ward. Macmillan.

A starving Japanese artist is commissioned to paint the death of Buddha. He longs to include his gentle cat, Good Fortune, among the animals, but legend says cats cannot enter heaven. Because of her goodness, he paints her, and the little animal dies of happiness. When the priest objects, the painting miraculously changes to show Buddha accepting the cat.

Honors

Mountains Are Free. Julia Davis Adams. Illustrated by Theodore Nadejen. Dutton.
Bruno, a young Swiss orphan who is being raised by the Tells, suddenly decides to become a page to an Austrian, saying he will return when he can earn his own way. The stirring of democracy causes conflicts as the Swiss try to rebel against the harshness of their Habsburg rulers.

Garram the Hunter: A Boy of the Hill Tribes. Herbert Best. Illustrated by Erick Berry, pseud. (Allena Best). Doubleday.
Hoping to find an ally for his chieftain father, Garram is sent to stay with the emir and becomes a favorite of the ruler. When he returns home, he discovers not only a plot to imprison his father but receives word that the eastern tribes are threatening.

Meggy MacIntosh. Elizabeth Janet Gray. Illustrated by Marguerite de Angeli. Doubleday.
In 1775 orphaned fifteen-year-old Meggy leaves her native Scotland to sail for the colony of North Carolina. There she joins Flora MacDonald, who had helped Bonnie Prince Charlie escape. Meggy becomes involved in the revolutionary cause and moves away from Flora, a loyalist.

Spice and the Devil's Cave. Agnes Hewes. Illustrated by Lynd Ward. Knopf.
At a workshop in Portugal, Bartholomew Diaz, Vasco da Gama, and Ferdinand Magellan gather to discuss their theory that an all-sea route around the Cape of Good Hope, also known as the Devil's Cave, must exist. The theft by pirates of the only known maps adds interest and intrigue.

Queer Person. Ralph Hubbard. Illustrated by Harold von Schmidt. Doubleday.
He can neither hear nor talk, and at age four he wanders into a camp of Pikuni Indians. His silence earns him the name Queer Person, and he is raised by an old woman in the tribe. During his test of bravery, he rescues the chief's lost son from the Crows, and it is revealed that they are brothers.

Ood-Le-Uk the Wanderer. Alice Lide and Margaret Johansen. Illustrated by Raymond Lufkin. Little, Brown.
An Alaskan Eskimo caught on an ice floe crosses the Bering Straight. After years of wandering, he returns home to establish trade between his tribe and the Siberian tribesmen. Once known as a weakling, after his hazardous adventures he is known to be a brave man.

The Dark Star of Itza: The Story of a Pagan Princess. Alida Malkus. Illustrated by Lowell Houser. Harcourt.
When the khan of Chichén Itzá kidnaps the betrothed of another Mayan chieftain, war breaks out, and the city falls into the hands of the Toltecs. The seventeen-year-old daughter of Chichén Itzá's chief priest agrees to be the sacrifice that will save her city, but her father bravely finds a way to save her.

Floating Island. Anne Parrish. Harper.
All packed up and on board a ship bound for the tropics, a doll family and their doll house land on Floating Island after their ship wrecks. They adapt well to the island but soon realize that dolls can never be happy if they are away from children for too long. They then arrange their own rescue.

1930 AWARD

Hitty, Her First Hundred Years. Rachel Field. Illustrated by Dorothy P. Lathrop. Macmillan.

Carved from a block of mountain ash a hundred years before, the six-and-a-half-inch doll now sits secure in the antique shop window and writes her memoirs. She recounts the adventures she had with many different people in places around the world. Illustrations show Hitty in many styles of clothing in her life thus far.

Honors

Vaino. Julia Davis Adams. Illustrated by Lempi Ostman. Dutton.
Ancient legends of Finland, the lives of three children, and the Finnish Revolution of 1917 are blended together to tell a story filled with strong patriotic spirit. Vaino and his older brother and sister become a part of the revolution that finally frees Finland of foreign domination.

A Daughter of the Seine: The Life of Madame Roland. Jeanette Eaton. Harper.
Madame Roland's life coincides with the French Revolution. The historical biography describes the childhood, married life, and tragic execution by guillotine of this remarkable woman. Madame Roland is intelligent and strongly supports the revolution, and her salon is depicted as the headquarters of much political activity.

The Jumping-Off Place. Marian Hurd McNeely. Illustrated by William Siegel. Longmans.
When the uncle who cared for them dies, four children pull up stakes in Wisconsin and move to South Dakota. There they weather adventures, hardships, and squatters for the fourteen months it takes to make homesteaders owners of the land.

Pran of Albania. Elizabeth Miller. Illustrated by Maud and Miska Petersham. Doubleday.
In post–World War I Albania amidst a threat of attack from Slavs, fourteen-year-old Pran falls in love. Rather than submit to an arranged marriage, she vows to never marry. After a truce is made, Pran realizes the man she loves is the same man her parents had arranged for her to marry.

Little Blacknose. Hildegarde Swift. Illustrated by Lynd Ward. Harcourt.
Little Blacknose is none other than the DeWitt Clinton Engine, the first locomotive built for the New York Central Railway. The personified engine tells of his life until he becomes enthroned in New York's Grand Central Terminal.

The Tangle-Coated Horse and Other Tales. Ella Young. Illustrated by Vera Bock. Longmans.
The Fionn Saga, the stories of Finn McCool known in every Gaelic-speaking part of Scotland and all over Ireland, is retold with vigor. The stories begin when McCool is a small boy learning about his heritage and his crafts and end three hundred years later when his son returns from the country of the Ever-Young.

1929 AWARD   **The Trumpeter of Krakow.** Eric P. Kelly. Illustrated
by Angela Pruszynska. Macmillan.
For two hundred years the Charnetski family has guarded
Poland's most famous jewel. When the czar of Russia finds
out about the valuable crystal, he sends men to steal it before
Charnetski's can get it to the king of Poland. Adventure,
mystery, and self-sacrifice fill this medieval story set in
Krakow.

Honors   **The Pigtail of Ah Lee Ben Loo.** John Bennett. Longmans.
Many original stories in prose and verse, and one brief
wordless story, are illustrated with two hundred intriguing
and often funny silhouettes. The stories are filled with
robust and irreverent humor: King Arthur's Sir Launcelot is
called "Sir Launcelot de Id-i-otte"! Most of the stories first
appeared in *St. Nicholas Magazine.*

Millions of Cats. Wanda Gäg. Coward.
A lonely old couple decides to get a cat. Searching for the
prettiest one out of a whole hillside filled with cats, the man
comes home with "hundreds of cats, thousands of cats,
millions and billions and trillions of cats." When the cats
fight about who is prettiest, only one is left.

The Boy Who Was. Grace Hallock. Illustrated by Harrie
Wood. Dutton.
In 1927 Nino the goatherd shows an artist the wooden
figures he has carved of famous Mediterranean people and
proceeds to tell their stories, covering more than 3,000 years
of history. He begins with tales of Odysseus, Pompeii, and
the Crusades and then goes through the nineteenth century,
occasionally including himself in the stories.

Clearing Weather. Cornelia Meigs. Illustrated by Frank
Dobias. Little, Brown.
It is just after the American Revolution and the economy has
not recovered. When young Nicholas Drury takes over his
family's shipbuilding business, he struggles hard until the
family fortune reverses itself with the successful design,
construction, and voyage of the *Jocasta,* a forerunner of the
clipper ship.

Runaway Papoose. Grace Moon. Illustrated by Carl Moon.
Doubleday.
Little Nah-tee runs away when outlaw Indians attack her
family's camp. Her parents cannot find her and move on with
the others. Nah-tee and a young shepherd boy she meets have
many adventures as they cross the mesa in search of her parents.

Tod of the Fens. Elinor Whitney. Illustrated by Warwick Goble. Macmillan.
Fifteenth-century Boston, England, is the setting for the amusing tale of Tod, who lives with a band of men just outside of town. Prince Hal, later to become Henry V, roves about the town in various disguises. Tod, realizing what is happening, tells no one and plays along with the game that is afoot.

1928 AWARD

Gay Neck, the Story of a Pigeon. Dhan Gopal Mukerji. Dutton.
Born in Calcutta, Gay Neck has thrilling adventures, first traveling all over India and later working as a carrier pigeon for the Indian Army in France during World War I. Eventually he returns to his young owner in India. Sometimes the story is told by Mukerji and at other times by Gay Neck the pigeon.

Honors

Downright Dencey. Caroline Snedeker. Illustrated by Maginel Wright Barney. Doubleday.
A Nantucket Quaker community during the War of 1812 provides the background for the story of a young girl named Dencey who first becomes involved with outcast Sammie when she hurls a stone at him. Ashamed, she tries to make amends but Sammie's trust must be won, and that is not easy for Dencey.

The Wonder Smith and His Son. Ella Young. Illustrated by Boris Artzybasheff. Longmans.
Fourteen stories of Gubbaun Saor, a mythological creature of Ireland, have been retold from tales the author heard from English and Gaelic storytellers. The stories capture the lilting cadence of the Irish language and are enhanced by the graphics.

1927 AWARD

Smoky, the Cowhorse. Will James. Scribner.
Born free on the open range, Smoky roams the hills until he is caught and gentled by Clint, a cowboy. Stolen and cruelly treated, Smoky kills his captor and runs as an outlaw. Captured again, he becomes a rodeo horse until once more he meets up with Clint and lives out his life on the range where he was born.

Honor

No record.

1926 AWARD   **Shen of the Sea. Arthur Bowie Chrisman. Illustrated by Else Hasselriis. Dutton.**

Sixteen charming and funny original stories are told in traditional folktale style. Most of the stories explain the origins of things like printing, chopsticks, and gunpowder. In several stories, the main character, always reacting the opposite of what is expected, is tricked by the smarter, minor characters.

Honor   **The Voyagers: Being Legends and Romances of Atlantic Discovery. Padraic Colum. Illustrated by Wildred Jones. Macmillan.**

Convinced that there is another land far away, Portugal's Prince Henry the Navigator gathers together all those who might know anything about it. In a high tower that overlooks the Atlantic Ocean, stories of legends and voyages are told along with those of the discoveries of Columbus and Ponce de León.

1925 AWARD   **Tales from Silver Lands. Charles Finger. Illustrated by Charles Honore. Doubleday.**

Nineteen stories that Finger gathered from South American Indian villagers are retold retaining their original flavor. Included are captivating tales of witches, giants, and strange enchantments.

Honors   **Nicholas: A Manhattan Christmas Story. Annie Carroll Moore. Illustrated by Jay Van Everen. Putnam.**

Nicholas, eight inches high, is a little boy from Holland who visits New York City for a few months in the 1920s. While there, he attends parties, visits famous landmarks, and learns about the Dutch influence on the city. His first party is at the library, where he is introduced to many book characters.

The Dream Coach. Anne Parrish. Macmillan.

The Dream Coach is pulled by one hundred misty horses. Helped by little angels, it travels the night sky dispensing dreams. Four children are introduced in turn, and their fairy-tale-like dreams, often involving inanimate objects that come to life, are shared.

1924 AWARD   **The Dark Frigate. Charles Hawes. Illustrated by Anton Otto Fischer. Little, Brown.**

A seagoing adventure turns sour when the *Rose of Devon* is seized in mid-ocean by pirates. The vile, ruthless men force nineteen-year-old Philip to be a part of the pirate crew, and the hangman awaits his return to England. Set in the time of King Charles, the story does not romanticize piracy.

Honor No record.

1923 AWARD **The Voyages of Doctor Dolittle.** Hugh Lofting. Lippincott.

Fun and nonsense reign as Dr. John Dolittle, a medical doctor and naturalist who has the ability to talk to animals, sets sail for Spider Monkey Island. There he unites two tribes, becomes king, and sails home inside the 70,000 year-old great glass sea snail. The story is told by the doctor's nine-and-a-half-year-old assistant.

Honor No record.

1922 AWARD **The Story of Mankind.** Hendrik Willem van Loon. Liveright.

Speaking directly to the reader, the author provides a fascinating picture of history from cave peoples to the present (1920). Ideas, movements, and people are more important than dates, and history is shown as something that builds upon itself.

Honors **The Old Tobacco Shop: A True Account of What Befell a Little Boy in Search of Adventure.** William Bowen. Illustrated by Reginald Birch. Macmillan.
Fred is befriended by the hunchback who runs the tobacco shop. Warned never to smoke the magic tobacco in the porcelain jar shaped like a "Chinaman's head," Fred stays away from it for a long time. One day he falters and suddenly finds himself involved in high adventure on the Spanish Main.

The Golden Fleece and the Heroes Who Lived before Achilles. Padraic Colum. Illustrated by Willy Pogany. Macmillan.
The ancient triumphs and tragedies of the Greek myths are woven through the central story of Jason and his quest for the Golden Fleece. The many stories told by Orpheus to the sailors in the story might be the very ones that the Argonauts heard on their long voyage.

The Great Quest. Charles Hawes. Illustrated by George Varian. Little, Brown.
Twelve-year-old Josiah tells of how his Uncle Seth is tricked by an old friend into selling his shop and buying a ship.

Thinking they are going in search of gold, Josiah and his uncle find themselves unwillingly involved in the slave trade and at odds with the crew.

Cedric the Forester. Bernard Marshall. Appleton.
Cedric, son of a thirteenth-century forester, saves Sir Richard's son and is made his squire. Taught to read and fight, Cedric becomes the best crossbowman in England, and, at the Battle of the Eagles, he is knighted.

The Windy Hill. Cornelia Meigs. Macmillan.
A brother and sister visit their older cousin in New England. Their cousin was once jovial but is now mysteriously irritable and preoccupied. A chance meeting with the beeman leads to their hearing stories about their own family's history. As they listen, the two children start to understand the cause of their cousin's anxiety.

The Caldecott Winners

1992–1938

TUESDAY

DAVID WIESNER

1992 Caldecott Award

Tuesday. David Wiesner. Clarion Books.

Flying frogs on lily pads move through the fen to a realistic small town on a Tuesday evening. They fly past a midnight snacker and a dozing TV viewer until sunrise when the lily pads dry and the frogs drop to the ground, hopping back to the pond. The fantasy ends with a comic twist suggesting more fantastic flights next Tuesday.

"Wiesner's watercolor illustrations show masterful use of light and dark, alternating perspectives and variation in page design, enabling visual storytelling in this nine-word book," said Mary Lou White, Caldecott Award Selection Committee chair.

1992 Honor Book

Tar Beach. Faith Ringgold. Crown Publishers, Inc., a Random House Co.

"Child Cassie flies high above New York City in the 1930s, high above the quilt squares that ground each page, high above the busyness and conflict of everyday life, from family rooftop picnics to daddy's construction work—*Tar Beach* has a folk art quality," said White. "The quilt form itself represents a historically important African American communication medium. Acrylic paintings on canvas paper form the basis of this visual feast celebrating the act of transformation—from the ordinary to the extraordinary, from earthbound, frenetic cry of life to free flight in the evening sky."

1991 AWARD   **Black and White.** David Macaulay. Houghton.

Macaulay interweaves fantasy and reality in a tale of parents, trains, and cows. The author recommends careful inspection of words and pictures to both minimize and enhance confusion.

Honors   **Puss in Boots.** Fred Marcellino. di Capua/Farrar.

Large pale type and golden toned paintings work brilliantly together providing an elegant regal look to the familiar fairy tale of Puss. With varied perspectives and points of view, Marcellino recreates the French court and countryside to ingenious, often droll, effect.

"More, More, More," Said the Baby: 3 Love Stories. Vera B. Williams. Greenwillow.

Brightly framed gouache paintings reflect each child's sense of security and joy as a loving adult "catches" that baby up. This creative use of color, shape, and rhythm marks a unique and distinctive celebration of family life.

1990 AWARD   **Lon Po Po: A Red-Riding Hood Story from China.** Ed Young. Philomel.

Suspense and drama are lightened with bits of humor as the wolf Lon Po Po tries to trick three children into letting him into their house. Though he succeeds, the children quickly turn the tables on the wily animal. The artist uses vivid watercolors and pastels to create dramatic panel pictures.

Honors   **Color Zoo.** Lois Ehlert. Lippincott.

Vibrant colors and overlays of geometric-shaped cutouts in heavy paper combine to create expressive animal faces. The text is simply a one-word identification of the shape or animal. All of the action is in the creative paper engineering.

Hershel and the Hanukkah Goblins. Eric Kimmel. Illustrated by Trina Schart Hyman. Holiday House.

Eight goblins haunt the old synagogue, preventing the villagers from celebrating Hanukkah until Hershel arrives to outwit all of the creatures. The dark illustrations are charged with energy as they show the imaginatively wicked goblins trying to frighten Hershel away.

Bill Peet: An Autobiography. Bill Peet. Houghton.

From the time he learned to manipulate a crayon, drawing has been a consuming passion for Bill Peet. He tells how that passion affected his life, from childhood, through his work at the Disney Studios, to his life as an author. Using his usual artistic style, Peet has filled his autobiography with new black-and-white illustrations.

The Talking Eggs. Robert D. San Souci. Illustrated by Jerry Pinkney. Dial.
Running away from her angry mother and spoiled sister, Blanche is befriended by a strange old woman who owns a cow with two heads and chickens that lay talking eggs. The eerie and suspenseful black folktale is filled with watercolor pictures of deep woods and strange sights.

1989 AWARD

Song and Dance Man. Karen Ackerman. Illustrated by Stephen Gammell. Knopf.

When his grandchildren come to visit, Grandpa whisks them up to the attic, where he performs an exciting vaudeville routine. The colored-pencil sketches are alive with movement and drama.

Honors

Mirandy and Brother Wind. Patricia C. McKissack. Illustrated by Jerry Pinkney. Knopf.
A sparkling, energetic Mirandy vows to dance with the wind at her first cakewalk — but to do that, she must catch it first. Lush, expansive illustrations of the rural South capture the vigor and imagination of the story.

Goldilocks and the Three Bears. Illustrated by James Marshall. Dial.
The antithesis of the typical sweet, demure Goldilocks, this little girl with her bouncing golden ringlets is brash, irreverent and captivating. Set in the present day, the briefly told nursery story abounds with color, humor, and wit.

The Boy of the Three-Year Nap. Diane Snyder. Illustrated by Allen Say. Houghton.
Taro has earned his nickname because of his laziness and penchant for sleeping. When he turns trickster to stop his industrious mother's nagging, she in turn outwits him. The handsome pictures are noticeably influenced by eighteenth-century Japanese woodcuts and reflect the culture of the land where this folktale originated.

Free Fall. Illustrated by David Wiesner. Lothrop.
In a book made more powerful because it has no words to stifle the imagination, a boy falls asleep and dreams of fantastic adventures. In this visual story, the objects around the boy evolve from one thing into another and then back to their original shapes.

1988 AWARD

Owl Moon. Jane Yolen. Illustrated by John Schoenherr. Philomel.

Late one quiet winter's night, a little girl and her father go owling, watching and listening for the signs that say a great horned owl is nearby. Blue-toned color washes and simple landscapes create a frosty, magical night perfect for owl watching.

Honor

Mufaro's Beautiful Daughters: An African Tale. John Steptoe. Lothrop.

Of the two sisters, one kind and good, the other mean and deceitful, only one will be chosen to marry the king. Dramatic yet realistic paintings in lush, jewel-toned colors illustrate this folktale from Zimbabwe.

1987 AWARD

Hey, Al. Arthur Yorinks. Illustrated by Richard Egielski. Farrar.

Janitor Al and his dog are swept away from their apparently humdrum lives by a huge bird that takes them to what at first seems like paradise. Full-color illustrations provide florid scenes of that paradise.

Honors

The Village of Round and Square Houses. Ann Grifalconi. Little, Brown.

Pastel drawings are used to illustrate the story of the remote Cameron village of Tos where the women live in the round houses and the men live in the square ones so that each has a place to be together and a place to be apart.

Alphabatics. Suse MacDonald. Bradbury.

Brightly colored letters of the alphabet become acrobats as they twist and turn until they become the objects that represent the letters: *A* becomes an ark, *J* becomes a jack-in-the-box, *S* becomes a swan.

Rumpelstiltskin. Paul O. Zelinsky. Dutton.

When the proud father tells the king that his daughter can spin straw into gold, it is the tiny Rumpelstiltskin who actually does the spinning — for the price of the firstborn child. Golden-toned, full-color oil paintings in medieval style retell this tale based on an early Brothers Grimm version.

1986 AWARD

The Polar Express. Chris Van Allsburg. Houghton.

Dark, brooding illustrations with unusual perspectives set the mood for a magical and poignant train ride. It is Christmas

Eve when the young boy boards the train for a trip to the North Pole. There he receives a special gift from Santa Claus.

Honors

The Relatives Came. Cynthia Rylant. Illustrated by Stephen Gammell. Bradbury.

What a marvelous time is had when all the relatives come from Virginia for a visit! They crowd into the house, where there is much loving and hugging and breathing to do together! The pictures nearly bounce off the pages with all the love and happiness in this book.

King Bidgood's in the Bathtub. Audrey Wood. Illustrated by Don Wood. Harcourt.

When the court is in a dither because the king refuses to get out of the bathtub, only the young page knows what to do. Illustrations reminiscent of an opera stage setting show off the full glory of the court scenes.

1985 AWARD

Saint George and the Dragon. Retold by Margaret Hodges. Illustrated by Trina Schart Hyman. Little, Brown.

Lady Una and George, a knight of the Red Cross, must find and battle the terrible dragon that ruins the land. Hyman's illustrations tell the story dramatically, and the reader seems to look at the scenes through an iron-encased window.

Honors

Hansel and Gretel. Retold by Rika Lesser. Illustrated by Paul O. Zelinsky. Dodd.

In this book translated from one of the less-embellished versions of the classic Brothers Grimm story, the artwork dominates. Sometimes imitating sixteenth- and seventeenth-century Flemish art, sometimes adopting a romantic nineteenth-century style, the paintings are rich in color and detail.

The Story of Jumping Mouse. Retold and illustrated by John Steptoe. Lothrop.

Large, expressive pencil drawings help tell the tale of a field mouse's search for the Far-Off Land. Armed with courage and hope, the mouse overcomes many obstacles until it is transformed into an eagle. The text is freely adapted from an unidentified Native American "why" story.

Have You Seen My Duckling? Nancy Tafuri. Greenwillow.

In this almost wordless book, a duck asks the creatures of the pond if they have seen her lost duckling. Bright, clear illustrations show the adventuresome duckling, who is always seen a little hidden from but close to his mother.

1984 AWARD   **The Glorious Flight: Across the Channel with Louis Blériot.** Alice and Martin Provensen. Viking.

Once he sees a flying machine, Louis Blériot becomes passionately interested in building his own machine and is successful on his eleventh attempt. Based on a true incident in France in the early 1900s, the biography is illustrated with pictures of shifting perspectives and touches of humor and views of a family growing older.

Honors   **Ten, Nine, Eight.** Molly Bang. Greenwillow.
Bedtime becomes a favorite time as the countdown begins. In a lulling rhyme, all of the things in a little girl's room are counted. The quiet time shared between father and daughter is illustrated with warm colors.

Little Red Riding Hood. Retold and illustrated by Trina Schart Hyman. Holiday.
The familiar story of the little girl who goes to visit her grandmother subtly warns children not to talk to strangers. The detailed illustrations seem to place the setting of the story in New England.

1983 AWARD   **Shadow.** Blaise Cendrars. Translated and illustrated by Marcia Brown. Scribner.

Translated from the French poet Blaise Cendrar's work, this symbolic mood piece reflects stories told by African storytellers and shamans around a nighttime fire. Rich colors with black cutout accents create the visual image of the prowling, dancing, mute shadow.

Honors   **When I Was Young in the Mountains.** Cynthia Rylant. Illustrated by Diane Goode. Dutton.
The author affectionately recalls a childhood spent with her family in the Appalachian Mountains of West Virginia. Warm family scenes are filled with friendly, happy people. Many of the illustrations drift off into the mountain mist and bring a peacefulness to the recalled pleasures.

A Chair for My Mother. Vera B. Williams. Greenwillow.
After a fire destroys their home, a little girl, her waitress mother, and the girl's grandmother move into an apartment. They start saving all their coins for a big, comfortable chair for Mama and Grandma. The watercolor paintings have a suitably childlike look.

1982 AWARD   **Jumanji.** Chris Van Allsburg. Houghton.

Looking for something to do on a boring afternoon, Peter and Judy decide to try the strange board game they find in the park. Boredom vanishes as every space on which they land comes to life. Meticulously crafted black-and-white illustrations bring the game alive.

Honors

Where the Buffaloes Begin. Olaf Baker. Illustrated by Stephen Gammell. Warne.
Majestic, haunting, and moody gray-toned illustrations show Little Wolf on his journey to the sacred place where buffaloes are said to originate. The rich prose was first published in *St. Nicholas Magazine* in 1915.

On Market Street. Arnold Lobel. Illustrated by Anita Lobel. Greenwillow.
A nursery rhyme–like verse breaks into a celebration of all the wares — from *A* to *Z* — that a little boy purchases on Market Street. The illustrations, based on seventeenth-century French trade engravings, show brightly colored shopkeepers composed of their merchandise.

Outside over There. Maurice Sendak. Harper.
When Ida is not focusing her complete attention on her baby sister, the baby is kidnapped by hooded goblins and replaced by a baby made of ice. Elaborate paintings combine romantic and surrealistic effects and are filled with subtleties and symbolism.

A Visit to William Blake's Inn: Poems for Innocent and Experienced Travelers. Nancy Willard. Illustrated by Alice and Martin Provensen. Harcourt.
Lyrical poems written in the spirit of William Blake combine with captivatingly imaginative illustrations that reflect the staidness and the whimsy of the eighteenth century. Nancy Willard also won the 1982 Newbery Award for this book.

1981 AWARD

Fables. Arnold Lobel. Harper.
Twenty original, brief, and witty animal fables, each complete with a moral, expose human foibles. Each fable is faced with a full-page painting in soft, rich colors that show the droll animals at the crucial moment of the fable.

Honors

The Grey Lady and the Strawberry Snatcher. Molly Bang. Four Winds.
An old lady who, except for her hands and face, appears as a grey silhouette, buys a basket of strawberries and proceeds home, pursued by a strawberry snatcher. Interesting colors

and textures are effectively combined with negative grey shapes in this vivid visual hide-and-seek game.

Truck. Donald Crews. Greenwillow.
Bright colors and geometric shapes roll across the pages as a truck carries a cargo of tricycles to its destination. There is no text. From the loading dock, through intricate highway systems, past road signs, to a truck stop, in clear and stormy weather, the big red truck moves its precious cargo across the country.

Mice Twice. Joseph Low. McElderry/Atheneum.
Cat is very hungry and wants a nice tender mouse to eat, so he invites Mouse to dinner. Things escalate until even Lion and Crocodile are involved. It is Wasp who settles things in this funny tale that is enhanced through whimsical drawings.

The Bremen-Town Musicians. Retold and illustrated by
Ilse Plume. Doubleday.
Four animals, all unwanted, set out together to become musicians but instead end up outwitting a band of robbers. The Brothers Grimm tale is illustrated with glowing, subdued colors and rounded shapes.

1980 AWARD

Ox-Cart Man. Donald Hall. Illustrated by Barbara Cooney. Viking.

Clean, uncluttered paintings capture the flavor of nineteenth-century New England as a family's day-to-day life is mandated by the changing season. There is a strong sense of the passage of time and of the rhythm of life in this book.

Honors

Ben's Trumpet. Rachel Isadora. Greenwillow.
The mood, sounds, and rhythms of jazz pulsate through the illustrations as Ben sits on the fire escape and blows his imaginary trumpet to the jazz sounds eminating from the Zig Zig Jazz Club. Set in the twenties and illustrated with dynamic black-and-white drawings, this is the story of one boy's dream coming true.

The Treasure. Uri Shulevitz. Farrar.
A poor man dreams that he must go to the castle bridge and wait for something that will turn about his fortunes. Traveling far to get there, he learns that the treasure is under his own stove. Illustrations with softly glowing colors and a striking use of light depict traditional eastern European villages and countrysides.

The Garden of Abdul Gasazi. Chris Van Allsburg. Houghton.
Illusion and reality become blurred when the unruly dog the
boy has been tending runs away into the secret, foreboding
garden of a retired magician. The visual perspectives and
the play of light on the gray pencil drawings create an eerie,
mysterious feeling.

1979 AWARD

The Girl Who Loved Wild Horses. Paul Goble.
Bradbury.
The kinship is so strong between a Plains Indian girl and the
horses she has lived with since becoming lost in a storm, that
eventually she becomes one of them. Sharp, brilliantly
colored paintings sweep across the pages and are in perfect
harmony with the story.

Honors

Freight Train. Donald Crews. Greenwillow.
Large pictures of the different freight cars are identified by
name and by color. Soon the train begins to move into a blur
of colors as it swiftly goes on its way.

The Way to Start a Day. Byrd Baylor. Illustrated by Peter
Parnall. Scribner.
A vibrant sunflower yellow and other colors blend with
crisp, black lines to make effective use of symbolism in
celebration of the sun. Poetic prose tells how cultures
throughout the ages have sung to the new day's sun to
honor it.

1978 AWARD

Noah's Ark. Peter Spier. Doubleday.
The only text is the seventeenth-century Dutch poem, "The
Flood," by Jacobus Revius, that opens the book. The rest of
the book is a visual interpretation of Noah and his unbeliev-
ably difficult task of tending the animals on the ark. Careful
details and softly hued watercolors depict the story with
reverence, humor, and delight.

Honors

Castle. David Macaulay. Houghton.
Macaulay traces in text and drawings the step-by-step
construction of a fictitious thirteenth-century English castle
in Wales from its conception to its baptism by fire — a direct
attack by hundreds of Welsh soldiers. The complex engineering task is generously illustrated with detailed black-
and-white line drawings and diagrams.

It Could Always Be Worse. Retold and illustrated by
Margot Zemach. Farrar.

Crowded into one room with his mother, wife, and six children, a man goes to the rabbi for help. The rabbi's answer is to bring one animal after another to live in the house. Dynamic, earth-toned paintings with an eastern European look capture the humor of the rabbi's good advice.

1977 AWARD

Ashanti to Zulu: African Traditions. Margaret Musgrove. Illustrated by Leo and Diane Dillon. Dial.

Twenty-six different African tribal traditions and customs are introduced using the English alphabet as the vehicle. A border on each page frames the text and illustrations, where glowing colors mix with rich browns. The attention to authentic detail in each painting is remarkable.

Honors

Hawk, I'm Your Brother. Byrd Baylor. Illustrated by Peter Parnall. Scribner.

In a gentle story told in simple, poetic prose, a young Native American boy wants desperately to fly like a hawk. Spacious, clean, panoramic line drawings convey the yearning of the boy and the power of the hawk.

Fish for Supper. M. B. Goffstein. Dial.

This quiet story chronicles the simple daily routine of Grandma, whose life centers around fishing. The black-and-white line drawings are centered in a square border of white space.

The Contest. Retold and illustrated by Nonny Hogrogian. Greenwillow.

Realizing that they are both engaged to the same woman and each unwilling to give her up, two robbers compare their cleverness in thievery to see who deserves her. Large, colorful illustrations capture the flavor of the Armenian culture in this humorous folktale.

The Golem. Beverly Brodsky McDermott. Lippincott.

The somber Jewish legend of the Golem, a creature created from clay that becomes more powerful and terrible than the evil he was made to destroy, is re-created with high visual drama. Striking paintings, vibrant with deep, rich colors, are filled with symbolism and massive shapes.

The Amazing Bone. William Steig. Farrar.

On her way home from school, hapless heroine Pearl Pig finds an amazing talking bone. When the delectable piglet is waylaid by a debonair fox, the amazing bone saves Pearl. Sunny, fresh, springtime landscapes provide the background for the well-dressed characters.

1976 AWARD

Why Mosquitoes Buzz in People's Ears. Retold by Verna Aardema. Illustrated by Leo and Diane Dillon. Dial.

Mosquito tells Iguana a tall tale about yams that annoys Iguana so much that he puts sticks in his ears so he cannot hear such things. Thus begins a chain reaction tale of the West African jungle. Illustrations show highly stylized animals.

Honors

The Desert Is Theirs. Byrd Baylor. Illustrated by Peter Parnall. Scribner.

A spare, lyrical text tells of the relationship of the Papagos people to their environment — "we share . . . we only share." The paintings are dramatic and are reminiscent of the layers of colors found in sand paintings.

Strega Nona. Tomie de Paola. Prentice-Hall.

Strega Nona leaves Big Anthony alone with her magic pasta pot after telling him never to touch it. It is not long before he does, and pasta literally flows through the town. Characters in medieval costumes of pastel, jewel-like colors add to the humor of the story.

1975 AWARD

Arrow to the Sun. Gerald McDermott. Viking.

The son of the Lord of the Sun sets out to find his father in this adaptation of a Pueblo legend. On his way, he undergoes four trials to prove his relationship to the Sun. The stylized, strong geometric art vividly portrays the desert and its intense sun colors.

Honor

Jambo Means Hello. Muriel Feelings. Illustrated by Tom Feelings. Dial.

Letters of the alphabet are represented by words of the Swahili language. A brief explanation of the word includes cultural information of East African countries. Beautiful full-page illustrations further depict the cultures.

1974 AWARD

Duffy and the Devil. Retold by Harve Zemach. Illustrated by Margot Zemach. Farrar.

The Cornish version of Rumpelstiltskin has delightful twists. When the maid guesses the devil's name, everything that he has sewn turns to ashes. Lightly colored illustrations treat the story with grand humor, and at the instant the name is guessed, the Squire is left standing in the fields, naked except for hat and shoes.

Honors

Three Jovial Huntsmen. Susan Jeffers. Bradbury.
The three jovial huntsmen go a-hunting on St. David's day
and find nothing they want. But lurking in the beautifully
drawn forests, many animals are seen keeping a close watch
on the huntsmen.

Cathedral. David Macaulay. Houghton.
The single-mindedness and spirit of the people and their
step-by-step construction of an imaginary medieval cathedral are meticulously recorded as the author-illustrator
celebrates the lives and art of the craftsmen who built the
magnificent Gothic cathedrals.

1973 AWARD

The Funny Little Woman. Retold by Arlene Mosel.
Illustrated by Blair Lent. Dutton.

A little woman pursues a rice dumpling and is led into the
underground world of the wicked Oni. Her escape proves
she is a funny little woman. Illustrations convey the mystery
and humor of the strange world of the Oni as well as the
dignity of this Japanese folktale.

Honors

Hosie's Alphabet. Hosea, Tobias and Lisa Baskin.
Illustrated by Leonard Baskin. Viking.
From the bumptious baboon, to the primordial protozoa,
right down to the "ruminating zebu," the artist presents an
alphabet bestiary of ever-changing format where spiders'
legs stretch across the page and dashes of watercolor become
the eagle. This work is highly imaginative.

When Clay Sings. Byrd Baylor. Illustrated by Tom Bahti.
Scribner.
Illustrated with the designs found on prehistoric pottery
from the American Southwest, this tribute to artifacts and
those who used them evokes a reverence for an ancient way
of life. The earth tones and prehistoric designs dignify the
word images of the poetic text.

Snow-White and the Seven Dwarfs. A Tale from the
Brothers Grimm. Translated by Randall Jarrell. Illustrated by Nancy Ekholm Burkert. Farrar.
Strongly detailed illustrations in beautiful, soft colors evoke
the sweeping, medieval, magical romance of fairy tales.
Randall Jarrell translated the Brothers Grimm story of the
beautiful girl, the wicked, malicious stepmother, and the
sturdy, somber dwarfs.

Anansi the Spider: A Tale from the Ashanti. Adapted and
illustrated by Gerald McDermott. Holt.

The moon is in the sky because Anansi, the great African folklore hero, could not decide which of his six sons should have it. Bright, geometric designs, bold, stylized animals, and rhythmic speech patterns are based on the Ashanti culture.

1972 AWARD **One Fine Day.** Retold and illustrated by Nonny Hogrogian. Macmillan.

Punished by having his tail cut off when he drank all the milk in an old woman's pail, the fox pleads to have it sewn back on so his friends won't make fun of him. The old woman agrees to do it, but only after he has returned her milk. The subdued and uncluttered pictures reflect the humorous cumulative action of the Armenian tale.

Honors **If All the Seas Were One Sea.** Janina Domanska. Macmillan.

An old nursery rhyme, its rise-and-fall rhythmic text reminiscent of the action of ocean waves, is treated to splendid etchings boldly filled with swirling, geometric lines of clear colors. The many shapes of each etching make a whole picture and provide the rhyme with even more momentum.

Moja Means One: Swahili Counting Book. Muriel Feelings. Illustrated by Tom Feelings. Dial.

Numbers from one to ten are represented by words in the Swahili language. Handsome, muted-gray double-page spread paintings depict scenes from Africa and relate to the illustrative sentences.

Hildilid's Night. Cheli Duran Ryan. Illustrated by Arnold Lobel. Macmillan.

Hildilid hates the night and the creatures of it. She does everything she can to chase the night away. Pen-and-ink drawings composed of thousands of tiny lines add a moonlit quality to the pages. Only at the end, with the approach of dawn, does yellow come into the picture.

1971 AWARD **A Story A Story.** Retold and illustrated by Gail E. Haley. Atheneum.

Kwaku Ananse, the great African spider man, completes three almost impossible tasks to win the Sky God's box of stories to tell throughout the world. The woodcut illustrations use African designs.

Honors	**Frog and Toad Are Friends.** Arnold Lobel. Harper.

In five affectionate and funny stories, best friends Frog and Toad share simple adventures and experiences. They welcome spring, find a lost button, tell stories, and enjoy being friends. The expressive and droll illustrations are in gray, frog green, and toad brown.

In the Night Kitchen. Maurice Sendak. Harper.
Falling through the night and out of his clothes, Mickey lands in cake batter in the night kitchen. From there he goes to the dough, builds an airplane of it, and flies to the Milky Way. The dream-fantasy is carried out in a chanting rhyme and is illustrated with an adaptation of comic book art.

The Angry Moon. Retold by William Sleator. Illustrated by Blair Lent. Atlantic.
A legend of the peoples of Alaska is retold with vigor, using lavish, full-color illustrations that elaborate on original Tlingit motifs. When Lapowinsa mocks the moon, she is taken into the sky country. Her friend must overcome many obstacles before he is able to rescue her.

1970 AWARD

Sylvester and the Magic Pebble. William Steig. Windmill.

A collector of pebbles, Sylvester the donkey finds a magic one that grants wishes. Caught by a lion, Sylvester panics and wishes himself to be a rock. Full-color pictures show the seasonal changes and colorful characters of the story and extend its concern and gentle humor.

Honors

Goggles! Ezra Jack Keats. Macmillan.
While showing off the motorcycle goggles he has found, Peter is accosted by neighborhood bullies. Proving that smart moves are more powerful than brute strength, Peter and his friends outwit the older boys. Rich, dark, brooding colors of paint and collage are lightened with vibrant colors in illustrations that reflect the urban setting.

Alexander and the Wind-Up Mouse. Leo Lionni. Pantheon.
Alexander, an unappreciated house mouse, envies Willy the windup mouse because everyone loves and coddles him. After asking the wizard lizard to change him into a windup mouse, Alexander has a change of heart. Large, bold collages enhance the simply told story.

Pop Corn and Ma Goodness. Edna Mitchell Preston. Illustrated by Robert Andrew Parker. Viking.

With all the gaiety and drama of a folk song, this original
story is told in nonsense verse. Ma Goodness and Pop Corn
meet, fall in love, marry, build a house and a farm, have
children, and enjoy the good life on their "prippitty
proppetty." Watercolor pictures have a haphazard look that
adds to the rollicking fun.

Thy Friend, Obadiah. Brinton Turkle. Viking.
His large Quaker family teases young Obadiah because a sea
gull has taken a liking to him and follows him everywhere.
The drawings are warm and gentle and vary greatly in
perspective. When the sea gull fails to be seen for several
days, Obadiah finds that what he thought was a nuisance is
really a friend.

The Judge: An Untrue Tale. Harve Zemach. Illustrated by
Margot Zemach. Farrar.
Prisoner after prisoner excitedly tells the Judge about the
horrible thing that is on its way. The no-nonsense Judge
throws them all in jail. When the horrible thing comes,
poetic justice is done. Illustrated in watercolors and line
drawings, the robust, pinkish characters tell their cumulative
rhyming tale.

1969 AWARD

The Fool of the World and the Flying Ship. Retold
by Arthur Ransome. Illustrated by Uri Shulevitz.
Farrar.

Line drawings and watercolors in bright, glowing, jewel-toned
colors show the magnificent flying ship and the landscapes
and onion domes of Russia. In this old Russian tale, the
scorned and foolish younger son of peasants overcomes
tremendous obstacles and wins the hand of the czar's daughter.

Honor

Why the Sun and the Moon Live in the Sky. Elphinstone
Dayrell. Illustrated by Blair Lent. Houghton.
Long ago, so the Nigerian folktale says, the Sun and Water
were friends and lived on Earth together. When Sun invites
Water to visit, the resulting flood forces them into the sky.
Elaborately stylized African motifs and traditional patterns
are used throughout the book.

1968 AWARD

Drummer Hoff. Barbara Emberley. Illustrated by Ed
Emberley. Prentice-Hall.

"Private Parridge brought the carriage," begins the cumulative text that leads to "Drummer Hoff fired it off" and a big

"Kahbahbloom." Woodcuts show vibrantly colored old-fashioned military figures.

Honors

Frederick. Leo Lionni. Pantheon.
The other field mice scurry to gather food for winter while Frederick gathers warm thoughts. In the deep of winter when the food has run out, Frederick is called upon to share his supplies. Collages enhance this story that proves "we do not live by bread alone."

Seashore Story. Taro Yashima. Viking.
On an island where "the quietness of ancient times" is felt, visiting children are reminded of the old story of Urashima, a fisherman who saved the life of a turtle. In return, the turtle takes him deep into the ocean to a mythical land. Muted pastel drawings capture the mysticism of the Japanese story.

The Emperor and the Kite. Jane Yolen. Illustrated by Ed Young. World.
Djeow Seow was the smallest and least noticed of the emperor's children. When evil men come and snatch the emperor away, it is Djeow Seow and her kites who rescue him. Intricate paper cuttings provide great beauty and a sense of cultural heritage in this Japanese tale.

1967 AWARD

Sam, Bangs & Moonshine. Evaline Ness. Holt.
Sam, a fisherman's daughter, has a bad habit of making up stories. The little girl learns to distinguish the truth from "moonshine" only after her best friend and her cat nearly meet tragedy. The book's pictures capture Sam's confusion of fact and fancy.

Honor

One Wide River to Cross. Adapted by Barbara Emberley. Illustrated by Ed Emberley. Prentice-Hall.
The text of an old folk song comes alive on brightly colored pages printed with black woodcuts. Stylized animals come forth one by one, two by two, and so on up to ten in nonsense verse with illustrations of animals that cumulate in groups waiting to board Noah's ark.

1966 AWARD

Always Room for One More. Sorche Nic Leodhas, pseud. (Leclaire Alger). Illustrated by Nonny Hogrogian. Holt.

A man invites all passersby to share his house with his wife and ten children until the house finally bursts apart. The Scottish folk song is told in lilting verse and illustrated in a subdued, dreamy manner.

Honors

Just Me. Marie Hall Ets. Viking.
The little boy tries to imitate the hops, walks, and wiggles of the animals on his farm. But when he sees his father, he runs to him as only he can run. Black-and-white drawings have a charming rhythmic expression.

Tom Tit Tot. Retold and illustrated by Evaline Ness. Scribner.
In this English variant of Rumpelstiltskin, the heroine is a comic, homespun character. Woodcuts executed in brown, gold, black, and aqua capture the broad humor and Elizabethan tone of the story.

Hide and Seek Fog. Alvin Tresselt. Illustrated by Roger Duvoisin. Lothrop.
As thick fog settles down for a stay, the lobstermen cannot put out to sea, the vacationers grumble because they cannot do anything, and the children frolic and play hide-and-seek. Pictures and text describe how life becomes transformed in a dense, wet, lingering fog on the Atlantic seacoast.

1965 AWARD

May I Bring a Friend? Written by Beatrice Schenk de Regniers. Illustrated by Beni Montresor. Atheneum.

Invited to tea by the king and queen each day of one week, the child quite naturally asks if he can bring a friend with him. Each day he brings animals from the zoo, and not all are well behaved! In rhymed text and creative illustrations reminiscent of stage settings, the absurd story is told.

Honors

A Pocketful of Cricket. Rebecca Caudill. Illustrated by Evaline Ness. Holt.
One day a boy who delights in the countryside finds a cricket and takes it home for a pet. An understanding teacher shows him how to share his special love of the cricket with the whole class. Pictures portray the inquisitiveness of a young farm boy.

The Wave. Margaret Hodges. Illustrated by Blair Lent. Houghton.
Giisan, the wise and respected old man of the Japanese village, must act quickly to warn the villagers that they are in great danger. The relentlessness of the tidal wave is seen in the brown, gold, gray, and black prints on every page and is heard in the urgency with which the story is told.

Rain Makes Applesauce. Julian Scheer. Illustrated by Marvin Bileck. Holiday.

Each two-page spread contains a nonsense line that always ends with "And rain makes applesauce" and the accusation, "Oh you're just talking silly talk." Illustrations in rich but delicate colors have an almost surrealistic effect and add a sophisticated tone.

1964 AWARD   **Where the Wild Things Are.** Maurice Sendak. Harper.

Sent to bed without any supper, Max travels far to where the wild things are. Taming them with a special magic trick, Max suddenly longs to be at home. The pictures are full of movement and magic, and in several two-page spreads without text they are absolutely boisterous.

Honors   **Swimmy.** Leo Lionni. Pantheon.
Swimmy, a small, black fish, convinces a school of small fish to swim in the formation of a large fish, thus proving that in numbers there is strength. The watery world is filled with shapes, patterns, and colors.

All in the Morning Early. Sorche Nic Leodhas, pseud.
(Leclaire Alger). Illustrated by Evaline Ness. Holt.
Asked by his mother to take a sack of corn to the mill, Sandy starts on his way. With each animal or person he meets along the way, the cumulative rhythmic tale grows longer. The drawings, with their overlapping colors, place the scene in Scotland, where the old rhyme originated.

Mother Goose and Nursery Rhymes. Illustrated by Philip Reed. Atheneum.
Wood engravings, both serious and silly in approach, decorate nearly all sixty-six rhymes and proverbs included in this collection. Large print, generous margins, crisp and colorful engravings, and just one or two nursery rhymes a page encourage a lingering look at each illustration.

1963 AWARD   **The Snowy Day.** Ezra Jack Keats. Viking.

Peter has fun on a snow-covered day making tracks and angels in the snow, building a snowman, and even trying to save a snowball for later. Spare, colorful collage pictures capture the wonder of a small child's trudge through new snow.

Honors   **The Sun Is a Golden Earring.** Natalia M. Belting.
Illustrated by Bernarda Bryson. Holt.
People have always wondered about nature and have made up stories and sayings to explain natural phenomena. The

author's collection of ancient sayings from folklore is reproduced here. The drawings lend an effective ethereal spirit to the book.

Mr. Rabbit and the Lovely Present. Charlotte Zolotow.
Illustrated by Maurice Sendak. Harper.
A little girl seeks birthday present advice from the wonderfully lanky, long-legged Mr. Rabbit. As the two wander through beautiful pastel scenes, she explains that her mother likes colors. They discuss many objects that are of the colors her mother likes the best.

1962 AWARD

Once a Mouse. Retold and illustrated by Marcia Brown. Scribner.

The brief, carefully chosen text taken from a fable of ancient India tells of a hermit magician that changes a mouse into a cat, a dog, a tiger, and finally back into a mouse again. Illustrated in woodcuts filled with patterns, the overlaying of the gold, red, and black add even more dimension.

Honors

The Day We Saw the Sun Come Up. Alice E. Goudey.
Illustrated by Adrienne Adams. Scribner.
In this poetic science book, two children get up very early in the morning and see the sun come up. They watch their long shadows and see what happens to them later in the day. Illustrations are in appropriate colors — gray and shadowy in the early morning, bright and clear at noon.

Little Bear's Visit. Else H. Minarik. Illustrated by Maurice Sendak. Harper.
Little Bear thoroughly enjoys his visit with his grandparents and delights in the stories they tell. The brown, green, and black-and-white illustrations of the cuddly, loving Little Bear and his fully clothed grandparents are enhanced with fine crosshatching.

The Fox Went Out on a Chilly Night: An Old Song.
Illustrated by Peter Spier. Doubleday.
Alternating double-page spreads of full-color and black-and-white detailed drawings greatly extend the story told in the old song. The fox kills a duck and a goose, outruns the farmer, and dines with his wife with fork and knife while the ten little pups chew on the "bones-o." The musical score is appended.

1961 AWARD

Baboushka and the Three Kings. Ruth Robbins.
Illustrated by Nicolas Sidjakov. Parnassus.

Old Baboushka declined to go with the three kings in search of the Child. Now, every year at Christmastime she continues her endless, endless search. On her way she leaves gifts for children. Rich, four-color, angular pictures in primitive style adorn the Russian tale.

Honor   **Inch by Inch.** Leo Lionni. Obolensky.
An inchworm saves himself from being eaten because he is able to measure things — a robin's tail, a flamingo's neck, a humming bird's body. But when asked to measure the nightingale's song, the inchworm must think fast. The bright green inchworm inches its way out of sight through a collage of grass.

1960 AWARD   **Nine Days to Christmas.** Marie Hall Ets and Aurora Labastida. Illustrated by Marie Hall Ets. Viking.

Now that she is in kindergarten, Ceci is old enough to join in the *posadas* — part of the special Christmas celebration that begins nine days before Christmas. Anticipation mounts as Ceci chooses her own piñata. Soft, gray backgrounds with splashes of bright colors project the warmth and excitement of the Mexican tradition in an urban setting.

Honors   **Houses from the Sea.** Alice E. Goudey. Illustrated by Adrienne Adams. Scribner.
Soft watercolor washes combine with poetic text to set the tone of this quiet, informative story. Two children gather shells along the coast and talk about the various shapes of the shells. An introduction and afterword provide more scientific information.

The Moon Jumpers. Janice May Udry. Illustrated by Maurice Sendak. Harper.
When the sun goes down, the moon comes up. Four children calling themselves the moon jumpers joyfully play and dance under the moonlit sky before bedtime. Soft night colors add a mystic touch to the simple story.

1959 AWARD   **Chanticleer and the Fox.** Adapted from Chaucer's Canterbury Tales and illustrated by Barbara Cooney. Crowell.

The old fable of the proud rooster and the wily fox was retold by Chaucer in his *Canterbury Tales.* Cooney has adapted that version for children. The text is filled with descriptive language, while the illustrations, rich in color and strong lines, capture medieval times.

Honors

The House That Jack Built: La Maison Que Jacques A Batie. Antonio Frasconi. Harcourt.
An old cumulative nursery rhyme, told in English and French, is illustrated with brilliantly colored woodcuts. A review at the end of the text asks questions in English and provides answers in French.

What Do You Say, Dear? Sesyle Joslin. Illustrated by Maurice Sendak. W. R. Scott.
Absurdly funny and outlandish situations are presented, followed by the question, "what do you say, dear?" and the proper rule of etiquette. Blue, yellow, and black illustrations continue the hilarity, even though the rule is presented straightforwardly.

Umbrella. Taro Yashima. Viking.
Thrilled with the umbrella and red boots she receives on her third birthday, Momo impatiently waits out the days until it rains. How proud she is when she can finally use her new rain gear! The impressionistic illustrations are filled with brush strokes of red, blues, and yellows and reflect the Japanese culture.

1958 AWARD

Time of Wonder. Robert McCloskey. Viking.
McCloskey celebrates in prose and painting the island where he lives. The alternately quiet and boisterous moods of nature are peacefully or dramatically recounted. The children of the island explore and enjoy the changing moods as the intensity of the blue and green watercolors shifts with the changes in the weather.

Honors

Fly High, Fly Low. Don Freeman. Viking.
In a story of love, loyalty, and suspense, the pigeon Sid faces perils while searching for the missing Midge, their nest, and the big letter *B* where their nest is housed. Colorful illustrations reveal scenes of San Francisco.

Anatole and the Cat. Eve Titus. Illustrated by Paul Galdone. McGraw-Hill.
Mouse Anatole, a loving husband and caring father, bicycles through the streets of Paris each night on his way to work. When a cat arrives on the scene, Anatole succeeds where thousands of other mice have failed. Gray drawings with accents of red, white, and blue and a smattering of French words reinforce the setting of the story.

1957 AWARD

A Tree Is Nice. Janice Udry. Illustrated by Marc Simont. Harper.

Trees are wonderful: They give shade, are fun to climb, are great to swing from, and even give cats a place to hide from dogs. Illustrated with watercolors, this book is a celebration of trees.

Honors

Gillespie and the Guards. Benjamin Elkin. Illustrated by James Daugherty. Viking.
Gillespie sets out to fool the three haughty guards by the old trick of the obvious. Robust illustrations are filled with humor and point with pride to the little boy who outsmarts the smug guards.

Lion. William Pène du Bois. Viking.
High in the sky, in the place where animals are invented, the boss comes up with a wonderful new name for an animal — "lion." His difficulty in deciding what it should look like is depicted in a line drawing of his original idea of a lion, complete with feathers, fur, and fish scales.

Mr. Penny's Race Horse. Marie Hall Ets. Viking.
Mr. Penny promises his animals a ride on the Ferris wheel if they win enough prize money at the fair. In an attempt to make sure they win first prize, the animals cause chaos. The dark black-and-white illustrations of the farm and the fair are all set within a border.

Anatole. Eve Titus. Illustrated by Paul Galdone. McGraw-Hill.
Shocked and shaken when he overhears humans saying that mice are terrible and dirty, Anatole the mouse determines to give humans something in return for the food he takes. Red, white, blue, and gray illustrations alternate with black-and-white ones as they reveal the world from the perspective of a French mouse.

1 Is One. Tasha Tudor. Walck.
Simple verse and delicate old-fashioned paintings and drawings introduce numerals from one to twenty. Each page is bordered with charming drawings of wild flowers. Within the borders children and scenes from nature represent the number depicted.

1956 AWARD

Frog Went A-Courtin'. Retold by John Langstaff. Illustrated by Feodor Rojankovsky. Harcourt.

In this story based on an old song and written in snappy, rhyming couplets, a frog courts Miss Mousie, and soon the insects and small animals scurry about preparing for the wedding feast. Full-color illustrations alternate with black-and-white and frog green ones, climaxing in a state of confusion as the cat joins the feast. Music is included.

Honors

Play with Me. Marie Hall Ets. Viking.
Reaching out to touch the woodland animals that she wants to play with, the little girl finds that they all run from her. She sits very still, and one by one the animals come close to her. Repetition in the story is loosely carried out in the quiet drawings as the girl never strays far from the pond.

Crow Boy. Taro Yashima. Viking.
In a deeply sensitive school story, Chibi, a very shy boy, is taunted by his classmates for years. A new teacher takes the time to talk to Chibi and discovers his talents. Set in a Japanese village, the story is illustrated with brush strokes that reflect an economy of style.

1955 AWARD

Cinderella, or the Little Glass Slipper. Illustrated and translated from Charles Perrault by Marcia Brown. Scribner.

Freely translated from Charles Perrault's French tale, this story of Cinderella, her ugly stepsisters, the fairy godmother, and the glass slipper is enhanced with illustrations that fairly dance across the pages with pink and aqua colors and whispy black lines. The enchanting pictures capture the romance of the tale.

Honors

Wheel on the Chimney. Margaret Wise Brown. Illustrated by Tibor Gergely. Lippincott.
Storks come from Africa to build their nest on the chimney and live by the cool, green rivers of Hungary. When fall comes they fly south over towns, rivers, and bridges. The full-page paintings of the Mediterranean city, the pink flamingos, and the flock of white storks in flight are striking in color.

The Thanksgiving Story. Alice Dalgliesh. Illustrated by Helen Sewell. Scribner.
Events leading up to the first Thanksgiving celebration in Plymouth Colony are told with the Hopkins family as the focus. Flat, primitive color illustrations of people are interspersed with rust-colored silhouettes of objects important to the Pilgrims in their new land.

Book of Nursery and Mother Goose Rhymes. Illustrated by
Marguerite de Angeli. Doubleday.
Three hundred seventy-six rhymes are delicately illustrated
in this oversized book. A soft, cheerful tone pervades the
sketches, many of which were inspired by scenes of the
English countryside. A small sketch of a goose appears on
almost every page.

1954 AWARD　　Madeline's Rescue. Ludwig Bemelmans. Viking.
When Madeline is rescued from the river by a dog, the dog
becomes the heroine of the convent school. The girls love
the dog, but the trustees say it must go. Bright, irrepressible
pictures match the indomitable spirit of the little French girl.

Honors　　The Steadfast Tin Soldier. Hans Christian Andersen,
translated by M. R. James. Illustrated by Marcia Brown.
Scribner.
Five-and-twenty tin soldiers, all made from the same tin
spoon, look alike except for the last one made. He stands
firmly on his one leg. It is he who falls in love with the toy
ballerina. Their tragic story is enhanced with blue-violet and
red drawings.

Green Eyes. A. Birnbaum. Capitol.
An all-white cat with long whiskers and green eyes is about
to celebrate his first birthday. In simple text and drawings
reminiscent of the bold lines of children's art, the tale of
Green Eyes's activities in the four seasons that have just
passed unfolds.

A Very Special House. Ruth Krauss. Illustrated by Maurice
Sendak. Harper.
The little boy is blissfully happy as he tells of a house he
knows where he puts his feet on the table, bounces on the
bed, and swings on the door. It is a place where everyone
yells for more, and no one ever says "stop." Line illustrations seem to frolic across the page, and only at the end is it
revealed that the story is a triumph of imaginary play.

Journey Cake, Ho! Ruth Sawyer. Illustrated by Robert
McCloskey. Viking.
When there is only enough food left to feed two, not three,
the bound-out boy is sent on his way with a huge Journey
Cake. The cake breaks free, bounces down the road, and
soon animal after animal joins the chase until they all end up
where the boy started. Expressive illustrations provide the
feel of an American folktale.

When Will the World Be Mine? Miriam Schlein. Illustrated by Jean Charlot. W. R. Scott.
Little Snowshoe Rabbit is born in the spring. His mother spends much of the year protecting and teaching him. She gently shows him how to adapt to the world around him, and in that way the world becomes his. The lithographs in browns and greens show stylized rabbits and their view of the world.

1953 AWARD

The Biggest Bear. Lynd Ward. Houghton.
Humiliated because his family has the only barn that never has a bear skin hanging on it, Johnny sets out with his shotgun in search of a bear. He returns home with a live, cuddly, hungry bear cub that soon grows into a big, rambunctious, voracious bear. The illustrations are sensitive, strong, and robust.

Honors

Ape in a Cape: An Alphabet of Odd Animals. Fritz Eichenberg. Harcourt.
Bold, humorous, colorful pictures and short, nonsense verses combine to create a lively alphabet book. From the "bear in despair" to the "yak with a pack," there is wonderful fun and imagination on each page.

Five Little Monkeys. Juliet Kepes. Houghton.
Buzzo, Binki, Bulu, Bibi, and Bali are the little mischievous monkeys who, because of their irritating tricks, cause the other jungle animals to band together to punish them. Alternating pages of color and black-and-white illustrations show the stylized monkeys acting up.

One Morning in Maine. Robert McCloskey. Viking.
While clam digging with her father, Sally loses a tooth that falls amongst the pebbles of the beach. Large, dark blue lithographs depict the great pride associated with losing the first baby tooth. All the characters in the small Maine town enjoy Sally's joy.

Puss in Boots. Illustrated and translated from Charles Perrault by Marcia Brown. Scribner.
The youngest son inherits a cat and realizes that after eating it he will have nothing left. Crafty Puss in Boots tells his master to do as he says and all will be well, and indeed it is! Puss, with his fine red boots, is shown as a grand, swashbuckling character who takes command of all the folderol of a French court.

The Storm Book. Charlotte Zolotow. Illustrated by Margaret Bloy Graham. Harper.
A little boy watches in wonder as the day turns ominously gray and still, a storm approaches, and breaks forth. He asks

his mother questions and she replies with reassuring answers. Each two-page spread of text is followed by a double-page spread of illustrations, most of them showing a driving rain.

1952 AWARD

Finders Keepers. Will, pseud. (William Lipkind). Illustrated by Nicolas, pseud. (Nicolas Mordvinoff). Harcourt.

Two dogs find a bone. One saw it first; the other touched it first. Unable to decide who owns it, they bury it and go off to seek the opinion of others and in so doing almost lose the bone to another dog. The bold use of color adds spark and flair to the simple story.

Honors

Skipper John's Cook. Marcia Brown. Scribner.
Beans! That was the trouble. The Skipper's crew refuses to sign on until a cook is found who does not fix beans morning, noon, and night. Young Si is hired on. After he has fried his 259th fish, the crew wants to know what else he can cook. Beans! Illustrations capture the expressions of the crew — and of the pots and pans.

Bear Party. William Pène du Bois. Viking.
When the koala bears become very angry with each other, it is "the wise old bear who lives at the top of the tallest Eucalyptus tree" who decides what to do. The koala bears are shown dressed in all the finery of a masked costume party, while wonderful onomatopoeic words describe the sounds of the musical instruments.

Mr. T. W. Anthony Woo. Marie Hall Ets. Viking.
Pandemonium reigns at the cobbler's when his dog and cat fight each other, and then both chase Mr. T.W. Anthony Woo, the mouse. Sister and her parrot move in, and things go from bad to worse until the enemies band together to create peace. Illustrations are contained within borders and suggest the control the cobbler wishes he had.

Feather Mountain. Elizabeth Olds. Houghton.
At one time all birds were naked and pink and featherless. One day they ask the Great Spirit to give them coverings. Black-and-white and color pictures depict the birds as they scurry around finding just the right colors to blend with their habitats.

All Falling Down. Gene Zion. Illustrated by Margaret Bloy Graham. Harper.
So many things fall — petals, rain, apples, even Daddy's book when his head begins to nod. This quiet, reflective

book is illustrated with pastel colors. There is a surprise ending when Daddy tosses the baby in the air.

1951 AWARD

The Egg Tree. Katherine Milhous. Scribner.
An Easter morning egg hunt leads to the discovery of long forgotten decorated eggs. With them the family begins a new tradition. Pennsylvania Dutch folk designs border many of the pages; the colors found in hex signs dominate the paintings that interpret the story.

Honors

Dick Whittington and His Cat. Marcia Brown. Scribner.
Artistic linoleum block cuts have humor and charm. They illustrate a simple retelling of the folktale of the boy who was made wealthy because he listened to his cat.

If I Ran the Zoo. Dr. Seuss, pseud. (Theodor Seuss Geisel). Random House.
Young Gerald McGrew likes the zoo but knows that if he ran it he would make some changes. He imagines all kinds of fantastic beasts with wonderfully creative names and unusual shapes and habits. Zany, whimsical illustrations are perfect for the imaginative verse.

The Two Reds. Will, pseud. (William Lipkind). Illustrated by Nicolas, pseud. (Nicolas Mordvinoff). Harcourt.
Red, the boy, sets out to play at the same time Red, an independent cat, sets out for food. The sense of impending chaos mounts as each gets in trouble at the same time in different parts of town. Sparse line drawings with brilliant splashes of red add spark to the illustrations.

T-Bone, the Baby Sitter. Clare Turlay Newberry. Harper.
T-Bone the cat loves to sit. That is what makes him such a fine baby-sitter — until the day he awakens with a twinkle in his eye, full of mischief. Expressive illustrations show the baby's extreme displeasure when T-Bone is taken away to the country and his pleasure when he returns.

The Most Wonderful Doll in the World. Phyllis McGinley. Illustrated by Helen Stone. Lippincott.
Duley loses a new doll. Her imagination runs wild as she describes the lost and most wonderful doll in the world as she wants it to be, not as it is. The book is decorated with four-color and black-and-white illustrations and borders.

1950 AWARD

Song of the Swallows. Leo Politi. Scribner.

Honors

The bell ringer and gardener of the mission church in Capistrano tells Juan the history of the mission churches and of the return of the swallows every St. Joseph's Day. Pinks, grays, yellows, and greens in muted tones convey friendship and a respect for nature. Two songs are included in the text.

Henry Fisherman. Marcia Brown. Scribner.

To be a fisherman a boy has to be able to swim very fast in case a shark is near. As the day when Juan will be allowed on the fishing boat draws closer, sights and sounds of a childhood in the Virgin Islands are portrayed in brown, coral, yellow, and green.

The Wild Birthday Cake. Lavinia R. Davis. Illustrated by Hildegard Woodward. Doubleday.

Johnny is so excited about going on an adventurous hike that he almost forgets his friend's seventy-fifth birthday. On his hike he catches a wild duck and later gives it to his friend as a gift. Abundant on the pages are the yellows and greens of spring.

Bartholomew and the Oobleck. Dr. Seuss, pseud. (Theodor Seuss Geisel). Random House.

Tired of snow, fog, rain, and sunshine, the king wants something new to fall from the sky. What he gets is green, gooey globs of oobleck that threaten to destroy the kingdom. Comical illustrations in black-and-white become greener and greener as the oobleck spreads.

America's Ethan Allen. Stewart Holbrook. Illustrated by Lynd Ward. Houghton.

Brave and rebellious Ethan Allen is born in the wilds of the old colony of Connecticut. He grows into a rugged frontier hero who leads the Green Mountain Boys. The illustrations and writing style resound with patriotism and historical significance.

The Happy Day. Ruth Krauss. Illustrated by Marc Simont. Harper.

The woodland animals are all in their winter's sleep when something causes them to open their eyes and sniff. Suspense mounts as they all race toward the thing that has caused them to awaken. Black-and-white drawings portray joyous animals as they leap around a bright yellow flower — the first sign of spring and the only color in the book.

1949 AWARD

The Big Snow. Berta and Elmer Hader. Macmillan.

When they see the wild geese flying overhead, all the woodland animals scurry to get ready for winter. After the big snow they slowly emerge to find food. Black-and-white drawings are occasionally interspersed with full-color paintings.

Honors

Blueberries for Sal. Robert McCloskey. Viking.
On the same day that Little Sal and her mother go to Blueberry Hill to pick blueberries, so do Little Bear and his mother. Soon a mix-up in mothers occurs. Dark blue-and-white type and drawings promote gentle humor against the ruggedness of Blueberry Hill.

All Around the Town. Phyllis McGinley. Illustrated by Helen Stone. Lippincott.
Snappy rhythm of the text and splashes of color in the illustrations capture the gaiety and pace of city life. Each verse is about a city sight and the rhymes are arranged in alphabetical order, from Aeroplane to Zoo.

Juanita. Leo Politi. Scribner.
As Easter draws near, Juanita and her friends join in the parade for the Blessing of the Animals at the Old Mission Church. The text is lovingly illustrated and interspersed with some songs, making the warmth of a close-knit community in old Los Angeles come alive.

Fish in the Air. Kurt Wiese. Viking.
On their way to fly a great big kite, Fish and his kite are grabbed by a Tai Fung, or big wind. It sends them on a high-flying adventure. Colorful paintings portray the excitement caused when Fish flies over town and countryside.

1948 AWARD

White Snow, Bright Snow. Alvin Tresselt. Illustrated by Roger Duvoisin. Lothrop.

Slowly the snow begins to fall and the adults busy themselves preparing for it. The children revel in it. A dark blue background gives way to white as the heavy snow melts and spring breaks forth. Reds and yellows provide a cheerful balance.

Honors

Stone Soup. Marcia Brown. Scribner.
An inhospitable town refuses to help three hungry soldiers. When the soldiers decide to make a soup of stones, curiosity overcomes the peasants and they learn a lesson in cooperation. Orange and brown pictures portray peasant life in a long-ago French village.

Roger and the Fox. Lavinia R. Davis. Illustrated by Hildegard Woodward. Doubleday.
Roger wants to see the wild fox and tries many times before he figures out how to be quick and quiet enough to do it. The

pictures turn from the warm hues of fall to the cold blues of winter before patience and ingenuity finally pay off.

McElligot's Pool. Dr. Seuss, pseud. (Theodor Seuss Geisel). Random House.

Told that he is some sort of fool for trying to catch fish in McElligot's pool, Marco visualizes the possibility that the pool is connected to the sea. Wonderfully imaginative creatures with fantastic names swim across the pages of this story told in verse.

Song of Robin Hood. Edited by Anne Malcolmson. Designed and illustrated by Virginia Lee Burton. Houghton.

Eighteen ballads of Robin Hood, most traced back to their original tunes, are exuberantly presented in verse, music, and art. The five hundred verses are decorated in a style reminiscent of miniature drawings of the fifteenth century. Its words meant to be sung not read, the book provides an energetic and lyrical introduction to the famous Robin Hood.

Bambino the Clown. Georges Schreiber. Viking.

The full colors and excitement of a circus clown's act are experienced by a sad young boy whom Bambino befriends. Peter is invited into the clown's dressing room, watches him apply his makeup, and becomes a very funny part of the show.

1947 AWARD

The Little Island. Golden MacDonald, pseud. (Margaret Wise Brown). Illustrated by Leonard Weisgard. Doubleday.

The seasons come and go and little by little the small island changes. One day a kitten visits the island and discovers that it does not stand alone but is connected underwater to land. The moods of the mostly green and blue drawings change with the seasons.

Honors

Boats on the River. Marjorie Flack. Illustrated by Jay Hyde Barnum. Viking.

There are warships, ocean liners, rowboats, and many other boats on the river that flows by the city and out to sea. Full-color paintings show close and distant views of the boats.

Timothy Turtle. Al Graham. Illustrated by Tony Palazzo. Welch.

On the day Timothy flips over on his back, each animal tries to help him right himself. The wise frog tells the other animals that what they could not do as individuals they can do as a group. Action-packed drawings add tautness and humor to the tale.

Pedro, the Angel of Olvera Street. Leo Politi. Scribner.
Young Pedro, who sings like an angel, leads *La Posada*, the
Christmas procession, on Olvera Street in Los Angeles. For
nine consecutive nights he wears red wings and sings carols
of Christian pilgrims. The soft colors reflect the solemnity of
the procession. Music is included.

Rain Drop Splash. Alvin Tresselt. Illustrated by Leonard
     Weisgard. Lothrop.
A single rain drop splashes down. Soon it is joined by
others, and a puddle is formed. The puddle grows bigger
and bigger until the rain drops at last become the sea, and
the rain stops. The poetic patterns of the text and the
drenched look of the pictures provide a closeness to nature.

Sing in Praise: A Collection of the Best Loved Hymns.
     Opal Wheeler. Illustrated by Marjorie Torrey. Dutton.
Twenty-five perennially popular Christian hymns have been
arranged to simple piano scores. Most of the hymns are
accompanied by a laudatory story about how the particular
words or melody came to be written. Romanticized illustrations show pious children looking heavenward.

1946 AWARD

The Rooster Crows. Maud and Miska Petersham.
Macmillan.

A potpourri of the rhymes, jingles, and chants of American
children is treated to a variety of visual interpretations. Each
rhyme is illustrated with humor and rhythm.

Honors

Little Lost Lamb. Golden MacDonald, pseud. (Margaret Wise
     Brown). Illustrated by Leonard Weisgard. Doubleday.
When the little black lamb strays from the rest of the flock,
the little shepherd and his sheepdog go into the perilous
night in search of it. The mood of the story changes from
bright, frolicsome pictures of the frisky lamb to dark browns
that reflect the concern the boy has for the lost animal.

My Mother Is the Most Beautiful Woman in the World.
     Becky Reyher. Illustrated by Ruth Gannett. Lothrop.
When a little girl becomes lost, she describes her mother
with her heart not with her eyes. Colorful pictures reflect
the spirit of the old Russian proverb, "We do not love people
because they are beautiful, but they seem beautiful to us
because we love them."

Sing Mother Goose. Music by Opal Wheeler. Illustrated by
     Marjorie Torrey. Dutton.

Fifty-two of the most familiar Mother Goose nursery rhymes
have been arranged to original, sprightly music. The piano
scores and the rhymes are accompanied by illustrations of
children, many of whom are in late-Victorian dress.

You Can Write Chinese. Kurt Wiese. Viking.
In China in the 1940s, a classroom of boys receives a language
lesson. The teacher explains that there are no letters in the
Chinese language, only words based on ancient pictures.
Most of the book consists of large drawings of Chinese characters
superimposed on drawings of objects that represent the words.

1945 AWARD

**Prayer for a Child. Rachel Field. Illustrated by
Elizabeth Orton Jones. Macmillan.**

A child's bedtime prayer asks for blessings on things that are
familiar to small children with such lines as, "Bless other
children, far and near, And keep them safe and free from
fear." Brief lines of the prayer are illustrated with full-page,
reverent golden-toned drawings.

Honors

In the Forest. Marie Hall Ets. Viking.
With his new horn and paper hat a little boy takes a walk in
the forest, and along the way he meets storks, kangaroos,
bears, and other animals who join his parade. All disappear
when the boy's father comes hunting for him. There is a
strong contrast between the white figures and the black
forest backgrounds.

Yonie Wondernose. Marguerite de Angeli. Doubleday.
His father has promised him something very special as soon
as seven-year-old Yonie learns to handle responsibilities like
a man. Strongly depicted in the illustrations and the text is
the hard but cheerful way of life on an Amish farm.

**The Christmas Anna Angel. Ruth Sawyer. Illustrated by
Kate Seredy. Viking.**
In a story set in Hungary during the war, Anna longs for a
Christmas cake shaped like a little clock. The deprivations
caused by the war contrast with the happy family traditions
of Christmas. While heavy on text, the book has several
illustrations reflective of the folk culture.

Mother Goose. Illustrated by Tasha Tudor. Walck.
Seventy-seven Mother Goose rhymes are gathered together
in this small book. Many of the rhymes are familiar, but
some are those usually found only in complete works.
Quaint, soft-colored pictures abound on every page.

1944 AWARD

Many Moons. James Thurber. Illustrated by Louis Slobodkin. Harcourt.
After eating too many raspberry tarts, the princess declares that if she can have the moon she will be well again. The wisdom of the royal advisors fails. The common sense of the jester prevails. Washes of pinks and blues complement the whimsy of the humorous fantasy.

Honors

A Child's Good Night Book. Margaret Wise Brown. Illustrated by Jean Charlot. W. R. Scott.
Night has come and everything is going to sleep. Animals, children, and even engines are sleepy. The brief story ends with a prayer to bless and guard "small things that have no words." The repetitious phrases and drawings are designed to bring on drowsiness.

Good-Luck Horse. Chih-Yi Chan. Illustrated by Plato Chan. Whittlesey.
A lonely boy in ancient China creates a very small paper horse that he can hold in his hand. Magically the horse becomes real. Although the magician names it "Good-Luck Horse," the story proves that sometimes good luck is bad luck and vice versa. The adventures of the horse are re-created in the line and wash drawings.

The Mighty Hunter. Berta and Elmer Hader. Macmillan.
Little Brave Heart's mother tells him to go to school so he can grow up to be a wise leader, but he goes hunting instead. Each animal in turn tells him that there is a better animal to shoot. The bear chastises him for hunting for "fun," and chases him to school. The illustrations alternate between black-and-white and desert colors.

Small Rain: Verses from the Bible. Verses selected by Jessie Orton Jones. Illustrated by Elizabeth Orton Jones. Viking.
Brief Bible verses taken from the King James Version of the Old and New Testaments are illustrated with children doing everyday things — romping, playing, sitting quietly, sharing, running, crying, and sleeping. Each verse relates in some way to what the children are doing.

Pierre Pigeon. Lee Kingman. Illustrated by Arnold E. Bare. Houghton.
Seven-year-old Pierre has long been fascinated by the boat-in-bottle in the shop. Finally he purchases it, and before he gets it home he breaks it. Studying the broken model, he succeeds in figuring out how the boat got into the bottle.

Gray, green, and peach tones reflect a Canadian fishing village.

1943 AWARD

The Little House. Virginia Lee Burton. Houghton.

Built long ago far out in the country, the Little House is now surrounded by the city. Circular shapes abound in the illustrations and the lines of type. Bright, happy colors give way to dark, moody ones as progress overtakes the house. Light colors return when the house is moved to a new countryside.

Honors

Dash and Dart. Mary and Conrad Buff. Viking.

In simple, poetic text and mood-capturing sepia paintings, the first year in the life of two fawns is described. A great reverence for nature is felt throughout the book.

Marshmallow. Clare Turlay Newberry. Harper.

Oliver the cat lives a blissful life of eating and sleeping until the lady who takes care of him brings home a bundle of live, soft fur. Suddenly Oliver is terrified when he is confronted with a bunny named Marshmallow. The pictures show how their relationship grows until they both curl up together.

1942 AWARD

Make Way for Ducklings. Robert McCloskey. Viking.

Having hatched her ducklings and taught them to march nicely in single file, Mrs. Mallard decides to take them straight through Boston's busy streets to their new home in the Public Garden and pond. Sketchy brown drawings humorously show the ordeal the mallards face.

Honors

In My Mother's House. Ann Nolan Clark. Illustrated by Velino Herrera. Viking.

Daily life of the pueblo as seen through the eyes of the children is described in a rhythmic, simple prose. Many aspects of life — houses, food, clothing, and agriculture — are pictured. Tribal designs and pen-and-ink and color drawings depict the Tawa life.

Nothing at All. Wanda Gág. Coward.

Three orphan dogs, two visible and one invisible, are adopted by two children. It takes a jackdaw, some magic, and a lot of energetic work by Nothing At All to become Something After All. Intriguing, lightly colored lithographs show the invisible become visible.

Paddle-to-the-Sea. Holling C. Holling. Houghton.
In the Canadian wilderness, a young boy carves a canoe
with an Indian figure seated in it, then launches it from Lake
Nipigon. The text and illustrations are filled with information about the scenes the canoe passes, from the quiet
byways, to a sawmill, to a raging forest fire.

An American ABC. Maud and Miska Petersham.
Macmillan.
Familiar symbols, historic places, and legendary figures
form the basis of this patriotic interpretation of the alphabet.
Decorated in red, white, blue, and black, each letter provides
a brief lesson in American history. The strength and courage
of those who shaped America are visible in the drawings.

1941 AWARD **They Were Strong and Good.** Robert Lawson. Viking.

Writing of his mother and father and their mothers and
fathers, Lawson says they, like the ancestors of many others,
were never famous but were "strong and good" and helped
to build America. Line-and-brush drawings are sometimes
humorous but more often depict the strength and goodness
of the land and its people.

Honor **April's Kittens.** Clare Turlay Newberry. Harper.
After her cat has kittens, April must decide on the one cat to
keep. Illustrations of the black cats make them look fuzzy
and furry. Occasional touches of red add a dash of color.

1940 AWARD **Abraham Lincoln.** Ingri and Edgar Parin d'Aulaire.
Doubleday.

Well-known anecdotes of Lincoln, particularly of his youth
and prairie years, are recounted with strength and humor in
this picture biography. Lithographs in color and black and
white reveal details of American life in the 1800s.

Honors **Madeline.** Ludwig Bemelmans. Viking.
High-spirited Madeline may be the smallest of the twelve
little girls at Miss Clavel's school, but she is by far the
bravest. Lilting rhythmic text and simple, childlike paintings provide a tour of Paris and introduce a spunky heroine.

The Ageless Story. Illustrated by Lauren Ford. Dodd.
The story of the Christ Child is told through Gregorian
music, biblical text, and illustrations that are an adaptation
of illuminated manuscripts. The illustrations are a blend of
early Renaissance religious art in a New England setting.

Cock-a-Doodle-Doo. Berta and Elmer Hader. Macmillan. In a reversal of the story of the Ugly Duckling, a chick is hatched by a duck. The ducklings make fun of him, and soon the chick goes off in search of others like him. In alternating color and black-and-white pictures he faces several perils before landing in the hen house.

1939 AWARD

Mei Li. Thomas Handforth. Doubleday.

The New Year Fair is in the city, and Mei Li's brother has been told that he can go, but little girls have to stay home. Strong, bold line drawings present many aspects of Chinese culture and customs as they follow the irrepressible Mei Li, who sneaks off for a grand time at the fair.

Honors

The Forest Pool. Laura Adams Armer. Longmans. Glowing with the bright golden colors of South America, stylized pictures show two boys as they go in search of the iguana in the bell-flower tree. The boys ponder the animals that know so much but never reveal their secrets.

Andy and the Lion. James Daugherty. Viking. The old story of Androcles and the lion is retold in a modern setting. Andy signs out a book about lions from the library. The next day he comes upon a lion with a thorn stuck in his paw. Told and illustrated with robust tall-tale humor, the twists of the tale lead to a fine friendship.

Snow White and the Seven Dwarfs. Translated and illustrated by Wanda Gäg. Coward. In this little book the Brothers Grimm story of the vain, wicked stepmother, the seven dwarfs, and the beautiful princess is retold with much repetition. The black-and-white drawings are filled with rounded shapes that continue the repetitiousness of the story.

Wee Gillis. Munro Leaf. Illustrated by Robert Lawson. Viking. The Highland relatives want Wee Gillis to stalk stags with them. The Lowland relatives want him to tend the cows. After years of doing both, Wee Gillis has powerful lungs from calling the cows, and he has learned to sit very still from stalking stags — just the skills needed to play a bagpipe! Line drawings sparkle with humorous spirit.

Barkis. Clare Turlay Newberry. Harper. A bickering brother and sister squabble over the ownership of a new puppy and cat. They finally reach a solution that makes them both happy. Soft brown-and-black drawings of the winsome cat and dog are set against white backgrounds.

1938 AWARD   **Animals of the Bible, a Picture Book.** Text selected by Helen Dean Fish. Illustrated by Dorothy P. Lathrop. Lippincott.

The Old and New Testaments of the King James Version are the sources for thirty-one stories about animals. Black-and-white full-page illustrations include the flora of biblical lands and portray the animals with reverence.

Honors   **Seven Simeons: A Russian Tale.** Retold and illustrated by Boris Artzybasheff. Viking.

King Douda, wise, rich, strong, and very handsome, decides to marry a princess as beautiful as himself. To help him in his quest, he engages seven brothers, each of whom has a special skill that, by the tale's end, is used in a most unusual manner. Love triumphs in the end in this whimsically decorated book with neat color line drawings.

Four and Twenty Blackbirds. Compiled by Helen Dean Fish. Illustrated by Robert Lawson. Stokes.

The twenty-four nursery rhymes found here were culled from out-of-print books or "rescued from memories of older people." Most are long and filled with the jingling and sturdy humor of traditional nursery rhymes. They are illustrated with vigorous drawings in black and green. Simple music is given for those rhymes that have tunes.

The Media Used in Caldecott Picture Books: Notes toward a Definitive List

Christine Behrmann

Since 1938 more than one hundred artists have illustrated picture books that have won a Caldecott Award or been named Caldecott Honor Books. Each of these books has won the accolade because of the quality of its illustrator's distinctive style, a style that has evoked images and ideas in the reader's mind that remain long after the book is closed. As the book is reviewed and discussed, we talk much about the artist's imagination, talent, and unique eye. Mentioned less often is the physical process by which the images imagined by that unique eye come to life and the role of the artist's medium (paint, lithography, pen and ink, etc.) in that process. In the fifty years since the Caldecott Award was first given, there has apparently been no systematic attempt to list the media used to create the honored picture books. This is a loss, because it is scholarly information useful to the study of children's literature, and because it is a humbling and educating experience to see the care, skill, and sheer craftsmanship that go into the creation of a truly distinguished picture book. This article is an initial attempt to fill the void.

What follows must be a work in progress, as digging out this information is a process that involves not only library research, but also correspondence with the artist, editor, or art director, and with other collections. In some cases, the information may be lost forever because it was never written down in bibliographic descriptions, and the author and the publisher are no longer available to be questioned. It is heartening to note that some publishers, such as Dial and Greenwillow, are beginning to list—in the books themselves—the media used in creating the pictures. This practice will certainly aid in the appreciation of the picture book as art.

Reprinted, with changes, from *Journal of Youth Services in Libraries* (Winter 1988): 198–212.

Christine Behrmann was Children's Materials Specialist, Office of Children's Services, New York Public Library.

The data listed below are thus, in many cases, preliminary only. Guesses were not made. When hard data were not found, the entry was left blank, except for a question mark. No information was regarded as final unless it was found in two independent secondary sources (review, bibliography, catalog, etc.) or available from one primary source (book, artist, publisher, Caldecott citation). Information from only one secondary source was included but marked preliminary by a question mark in parentheses. Corrections and added information are earnestly solicited. The most important result is to obtain, eventually, a complete, accurate list.

Many deserve thanks for their kind cooperation thus far, but it is most important to single out Lyn Lacey, whose excellent idea this project was.

Year Award
1938 *Animals of the Bible*
    by Helen Dean Fish;
    Illustrated by Dorothy P.
    Lathrop (Lippincott)
    —black-and-white lithographs

1939 *Mei Li*
    by Thomas Handforth
    (Doubleday)
    —brush and lithograph pencil (?)

Honor
Seven Simeons
    by Boris Artzybasheff (Viking)
    —pen and ink
Four and Twenty Blackbirds
    by Helen Dean Fish; Illustrated
    by Robert Lawson (Stokes)
    —drawings in pen and tempera

The Forest Pool
    by Laura Adams Armer
    (Longmans) (?)
Wee Gillis
    by Munro Leaf; Illustrated by
    Robert Lawson (Viking)
    —drawings in pen and tempera
Snow White and the Seven Dwarfs
    by Wanda Gäg (Coward)
    —lithographs (?)
Barkis
    by Clare Newberry (Harper)
    —charcoal pencil and watercolor
    wash
Andy and the Lion
    by James Daugherty (Viking)
    —charcoal rubbed off on light
    gray transfer and rubbed in (?)

Year Award
1940 *Abraham Lincoln*
by Ingri and Edgar Parin
d'Aulaire (Doubleday)
—lithographic pencil on stone

Honor
Cock-a-Doodle-Doo
by Berta and Elmer Hader
(Macmillan)
—watercolor
Madeline
by Ludwig Bemelmans (Viking)
—brush, pen, and watercolor (?)
The Ageless Story
Illustrated by Lauren Ford
(Dodd)
—painting; touches of gold leaf
(?)

1941 *They Were Strong and Good*
by Robert Lawson (Viking)
—brush and ink

April's Kittens
by Clare Newberry (Harper)
—ink, charcoal, and watercolor

1942 *Make Way for Ducklings*
by Robert McCloskey (Viking)
—lithographic crayon on stone

An American ABC
by Maud and Miska Petersham
(Macmillan)
—pencil and preseparated
watercolor
In My Mother's House
by Ann Nolan Clark; Illustrated
by Velino Herrera (Viking) (?)
Paddle-to-the-Sea
by Holling C. Holling
(Houghton)
—full-color oil paintings
Nothing at All
by Wanda Gäg (Coward)
—original lithographs in color

1943 *The Little House*
by Virginia Lee Burton
(Houghton)
—watercolor

Dash and Dart
by Mary and Conrad Buff
(Viking)
—lithographs (?)
Marshmallow
by Clare Newberry (Harper)
—charcoal (?)

Year Award

1944 *Many Moons*
by James Thurber; Illustrated by
Louis Slobodkin (HBJ)
—pen and ink; watercolor

Honor

Small Rain: Verses from the Bible
Selected by Jessie Orton Jones;
Illustrated by Elizabeth Orton
Jones (Viking) (?)

Pierre Pigeon
by Lee Kingman; Illustrated by
Arnold E. Bare (Houghton)
—preseparated gouache and ink
drawings

The Mighty Hunter
by Berta and Elmer Hader
(Macmillan)
—watercolor

A Child's Good Night Book
by Margaret Wise Brown;
Illustrated by Jean Charlot
(Scott)
—crayon drawings

Good-Luck Horse
by Chih–Yi Chan; Illustrated by
Plato Chan (Wittlesey)
—pen and ink; wash (?)

1945 *Prayer for a Child*
by Rachel Field; Illustrated by
Elizabeth Orton Jones
(Macmillan)
—pen and ink; watercolor

Mother Goose
Illustrated by Tasha Tudor
(Walck)
—graphite and watercolor (?)

In the Forest
by Marie Hall Ets (Viking)
—paper batik

Yonie Wondernose
by Marguerite de Angeli
(Doubleday)
—color separations done in pen,
ink, pencil, and watercolor

The Christmas Anna Angel
by Ruth Sawyer; Illustrated by
Kate Seredy (Viking) (?)

1946 *The Rooster Crows*
by Maud and Miska Petersham
(Macmillan)
—lithograph pencil with color
separations on acetate

Little Lost Lamb
by Golden MacDonald;
Illustrated by Leonard Weisgard
(Doubleday) (?)

Year Award

Honor
Sing Mother Goose
by Opal Wheeler; Illustrated by
Marjorie Torrey (Dutton) (?)
*My Mother Is the Most Beautiful
Woman in the World*
by Becky Reyher; Illustrated by
Ruth C. Gannett (Lothrop)
—original gouache and
watercolor reproduced by
four-match process using
lithographic crayon
You Can Write Chinese
by Kurt Wiese (Viking)
—ink and watercolor separations

1947 *The Little Island*
by Golden MacDonald;
Illustrated by Leonard Weisgard
(Doubleday)
—gouache

Boats on the River
by Marjorie Flack; Illustrated by
Jay Hyde Barnum (Viking) (?)
Timothy Turtle
by Al Graham; Illustrated by
Tony Palazzo (Welch)
—black-and-white pen and ink
(?)
Pedro, the Angel of Olvera Street
by Leo Politi (Scribner) (?)
*Sing in Praise: A Collection of Best
Loved Hymns*
by Opal Wheeler; Illustrated by
Marjorie Torrey (Dutton) (?)
Rain Drop Splash
by Alvin Tresselt; Illustrated by
Leonard Weisgard (Lothrop)
—three colors preseparated with
india ink on acetate overlays

1948 *White Snow, Bright Snow*
by Alvin Tresselt; Illustrated by
Roger Duvoisin (Lothrop)
—acetate separations in black india
ink

Stone Soup
by Marcia Brown (Scribner)
—ink and watercolor (?)
McElligot's Pool
by Dr. Seuss (Random)
—pencil and watercolor
Bambino the Clown
by Georges Schreiber (Viking) (?)

Year Award

Honor
Roger and the Fox
by Lavinia Davis; Illustrated by
Hildegard Woodward
(Doubleday)
—ink (?)
Song of Robin Hood
Edited by Anne Malcolmson;
Illustrated by Virginia Lee
Burton (Houghton)
—scratchboard

1949 *The Big Snow*
by Berta and Elmer Hader
(Macmillan)
—watercolor

Blueberries for Sal
by Robert McCloskey (Viking)
—lithographs (?)
All Around the Town
by Phyllis McGinley; Illustrated
by Helen Stone (Lippincott) (?)
Juanita
by Leo Politi (Scribner)
—tempera (?)
Fish in the Air
by Kurt Wiese (Viking)
—ink and watercolor

1950 *Song of the Swallows*
by Leo Politi (Scribner)
—tempera

America's Ethan Allen
by Stewart Holbrook; Illustrated
by Lynd Ward (Houghton)
—full-color gouache paintings
The Wild Birthday Cake
by Lavinia Davis; Illustrated by
Hildegard Woodward
(Doubleday) (?)
The Happy Day
by Ruth Krauss; Illustrated by
Marc Simont (Harper) (?)
Bartholomew and the Oobleck
by Dr. Seuss (Random)
—pencil, crayon, and watercolor
Henry Fisherman
by Marcia Brown (Scribner)
—collage (?)

Year Award
1951 *The Egg Tree*
by Katherine Milhous (Scribner)
—tempera

Honor
Dick Whittington and His Cat
by Marcia Brown (Scribner)
—linoleum cuts
The Two Reds
by Will Lipkind; Illustrated by
Nicolas Mordvinoff (HBJ)
—acetate separations using pen,
ink, and brush
If I Ran the Zoo
by Dr. Seuss (Random)
—pencil, ink, and watercolor
The Most Wonderful Doll in the World
by Phyllis McGinley; Illustrated
by Helen Stone (Lippincott) (?)
T-Bone, the Baby Sitter
by Clare Newberry (Harper)
—pen, ink, and charcoal (?)

1952 *Finders Keepers*
by Will Lipkind;
Illustrated by Nicolas
Mordvinoff (HBJ)
—acetate color separations for
line reproduction

Mr. T. W. Anthony Woo
by Marie Hall Ets (Viking)
—paper batik
Skipper John's Cook
by Marcia Brown (Scribner) (?)
All Falling Down
by Gene Zion; Illustrated by
Margaret Bloy Graham (Harper)
(?)
Bear Party
by William Pène du Bois
(Viking) (?)
Feather Mountain
by Elizabeth Olds (Houghton)
—preseparated art and
watercolor wash (four-color)

1953 *The Biggest Bear*
by Lynd Ward (Houghton)
—opaque watercolor

Puss in Boots
by Charles Perrault; Illustrated
and translated by Marcia Brown
(Scribner)
—woodcut and watercolor (?)
One Morning in Maine
by Robert McCloskey (Viking)
—lithographs (?)

Year Award

Honor
Ape in a Cape
by Fritz Eichenberg (HBJ)
—woodcuts; acetate separations
The Storm Book
by Charlotte Zolotow; Illustrated
by Margaret Bloy Graham
(Harper) (?)
Five Little Monkeys
by Juliet Kepes (Houghton)
—preseparated ink and
watercolor wash (four-color)

1954 *Madeline's Rescue*
by Ludwig Bemelmans (Viking)
—brush, pen, and watercolor

Journey Cake, Ho!
by Ruth Sawyer; Illustrated by
Robert McCloskey (Viking) (?)
When Will the World Be Mine?
by Miriam Schlein; Illustrated
by Jean Charlot (Scott)
—lithographs (?)
The Steadfast Tin Soldier
by Hans Christian Andersen;
Illustrated by Marcia Brown
(Scribner) (?)
A Very Special House
by Ruth Krauss; Illustrated by
Maurice Sendak (Harper) (?)
Green Eyes
by A. Birnbaum (Capitol) (?)

1955 *Cinderella*
by Charles Perrault; Translated
and illustrated by Marcia Brown
(Scribner)
—gouache, crayon, watercolor,
and ink

*Book of Nursery and Mother Goose
Rhymes*
Illustrated by Marguerite de
Angeli (Doubleday)
—Sharp Wolf pencils and
watercolor
Wheel on the Chimney
by Margaret Wise Brown;
Illustrated by Tibor Gergely
(Lippincott)
—gouache (?)
The Thanksgiving Story
by Alice Dalgliesh; Illustrated by
Helen Sewell (Scribner) (?)

Year Award
1956 *Frog Went A-Courtin'*
Retold by John Langstaff;
Illustrated by Feodor
Rojankovsky (HBJ)
—brush, ink, and crayon on
acetate separations

1957 *A Tree Is Nice*
by Janice Udry; Illustrated by
Marc Simont (Harper)
—gouache over watercolor

1958 *Time of Wonder*
by Robert McCloskey (Viking)
—casein

Honor
Play with Me
by Marie Hall Ets (Viking)
—graphite separations
Crow Boy
by Taro Yashima (Viking)
—pencil and brush separations

Mr. Penny's Race Horse
by Marie Hall Ets (Viking)
—paper batik
1 Is One
by Tasha Tudor (Walck)
—graphite and watercolor (?)
Anatole
by Eve Titus; Illustrated by Paul
Galdone (McGraw)
—pen and ink with gray wash
over graphite with paper collage
(?)
Gillespie and the Guards
by Benjamin Elkin; Illustrated
by James Daugherty (Viking)
—charcoal rubbed off on light
gray transfer and inked (?)
Lion
by William Pène du Bois
(Viking)
—pen and india ink; color
preseparated on Dinobase with
lithographic pencil

Fly High, Fly Low
by Don Freeman (Viking)
—colored pencil accented by
outlines in ink
Anatole and the Cat
by Eve Titus; Illustrated by Paul
Galdone (McGraw)
—pen and ink with gray wash
over graphite with paper collage
(?)

Year Award

1959 *Chanticleer and the Fox*
Adapted from Chaucer and
illustrated by Barbara Cooney
(Crowell)
—preseparated art: black and
white on scratchboard; colors on
Dinobase

1960 *Nine Days to Christmas*
by Marie Hall Ets and Aurora
Labastida; Illustrated by
Marie Hall Ets (Viking)
—pencil on Dinobase

1961 *Baboushka and the Three Kings*
by Ruth Robbins; Illustrated by
Nicolas Sidjakov (Parnassus)
—tempera and felt-tip pen in
four colors

1962 *Once a Mouse*
by Marcia Brown (Scribner)
—woodcuts and watercolor

Honor

The House That Jack Built
by Antonio Frasconi (HBJ)
—woodcuts
What Do You Say, Dear?
by Sesyle Joslin; Illustrated by
Maurice Sendak (Scott)
—pen and ink with watercolor
wash separations
Umbrella
by Taro Yashima (Viking)
—watercolor; pencil and brush
for direct separations

Houses from the Sea
by Alice E. Goudey; Illustrated
by Adrienne Adams (Scribner)
—watercolor (?)
The Moon Jumpers
by Janice Udry; Illustrated by
Maurice Sendak (Harper)
—tempera

Inch by Inch
by Leo Lionni (Obolensky)
—rice paper collage and crayon

The Fox Went Out on a Chilly Night
Illustrated by Peter Spier
(Doubleday)
—pen and ink and watercolor on
blue boards
Little Bear's Visit
by Else Holmelund Minarik;
Illustrated by Maurice Sendak
(Harper)
—pen and ink with wash
separations
The Day We Saw the Sun Come Up
by Alice E. Goudey; Illustrated
by Adrienne Adams (Scribner)
—graphite and gray wash with
white gouache separations

Year Award

1963 *The Snowy Day*
by Ezra Jack Keats (Viking)
—collage: papers, paints, and gum-eraser stamps

1964 *Where the Wild Things Are*
by Maurice Sendak (Harper)
—india ink line over full-color tempera

1965 *May I Bring a Friend?*
by Beatrice Schenk de Regniers;
Illustrated by Beni Montresor
(Atheneum)
—pen-and-ink drawings on board in black with solid overlays and screened overlays on acetate

1966 *Always Room for One More*
by Sorche Nic Leodhas;
Illustrated by Nonny Hogrogian
(Holt)
—three-color preseparated art using pen for black line and pastels and wash for color

Honor

The Sun Is a Golden Earring
by Natalia M. Belting;
Illustrated by Bernarda Bryson
(Holt)
—pencil
Mr. Rabbit and the Lovely Present
by Charlotte Zolotow; Illustrated by Maurice Sendak (Harper)
—watercolor

Swimmy
by Leo Lionni (Pantheon)
—watercolor, rubber stamping, and pencil
All in the Morning Early
by Sorche Nic Leodhas;
Illustrated by Evaline Ness
(Holt) (?)
Mother Goose and Nursery Rhymes
Illustrated by Philip Reed
(Atheneum)
—engravings on wood

Rain Makes Applesauce
by Julian Scheer; Illustrated by Marvin Bileck (Holiday)
—pencil and watercolors (?)
The Wave
by Margaret Hodges; Illustrated by Blair Lent (Houghton)
—ink and cardboard cutouts
A Pocketful of Cricket
by Rebecca Caudill; Illustrated by Evaline Ness (Holt) (?)

Hide and Seek Fog
by Alvin Tresselt; Illustrated by Roger Duvoisin (Lothrop)
—full-color gouache
Just Me
by Marie Hall Ets (Viking)
—paper batik

Year Award

Honor
Tom-Tit-Tot
   by Evaline Ness (Holt)
   —woodcuts

1967 *Sam, Bangs & Moonshine*
   by Evaline Ness (Holt)
   —three-color preseparated art
   using Japanese pen and wash;
   printer's ink; roller; string

One Wide River to Cross
   by Barbara Emberley; Illustrated
   by Ed Emberley (Prentice)
   —woodcuts

1968 *Drummer Hoff*
   by Barbara Emberley;
   Illustrated by Ed Emberley
   (Prentice)
   —woodcuts and ink

Frederick
   by Leo Lionni (Pantheon)
   —collage with mixed media
Seashore Story
   by Taro Yashima (Viking)
   —watercolor and pastel
The Emperor and the Kite
   by Jane Yolen; Illustrated by Ed
   Young (World)
   —paper cuts

1969 *The Fool of the World and the
   Flying Ship*
   Retold by Arthur Ransome;
   Illustrated by Uri Shulevitz
   (Farrar)
   —pen and brush with black and
   colored inks

*Why the Sun and the Moon Live in the
   Sky*
   by Elphinstone Dayrell;
   Illustrated by Blair Lent
   (Houghton)
   —preseparated pen and ink in
   three colors

1970 *Sylvester and the Magic Pebble*
   by William Steig (Windmill)
   —watercolor

Goggles!
   by Ezra Jack Keats (Macmillan)
   —oil paint and collage
Alexander and the Wind-Up Mouse
   by Leo Lionni (Pantheon)
   —collage
Pop Corn and Ma Goodness
   by Edna Mitchell Preston;
   Illustrated by Robert Andrew
   Parker (Viking)
   —watercolor
Thy Friend, Obadiah
   by Brinton Turkle (Viking) (?)

Year Award

Honor
The Judge
　by Harve Zemach; Illustrated by
　Margot Zemach (Farrar)
　—watercolor, pen and ink

1971 *A Story A Story*
　by Gail E. Haley (Atheneum)
　—woodcuts

The Angry Moon
　by William Sleator; Illustrated
　by Blair Lent (Atlantic/Little)
　—pen-and-ink drawings with
　acrylic glazes; full-color paintings
Frog and Toad Are Friends
　by Arnold Lobel (Harper)
　—pencil drawings in three colors
In the Night Kitchen
　by Maurice Sendak (Harper)
　—line drawings and wash

1972 *One Fine Day*
　by Nonny Hogrogian
　(Macmillan)
　—acrylic paintings with
　turpentine on gesso panels

Hildilid's Night
　by Cheli Duran Ryan; Illustrated
　by Arnold Lobel (Macmillan)
　—pen-and-ink drawings with
　yellow overlays
If All the Seas Were One Sea
　by Janina Domanska
　(Macmillan)
　—etchings on zinc plates with
　brush-and-ink overlays
Moja Means One
　by Muriel Feelings; Illustrated
　by Tom Feelings (Dial)
　—graphite and paper collage

1973 *The Funny Little Woman*
　by Arlene Mosel; Illustrated by
　Blair Lent (Dutton)
　—pen-and-ink line drawings with
　full-color acrylic glazes; full-color
　paintings

Anansi the Spider
　Adapted and illustrated by Gerald
　McDermott (Holt)
　—artwork preseparated in four
　colors with outline in ink
Hosie's Alphabet
　by Hosea, Tobias, and Lisa
　Baskin; Illustrated by Leonard
　Baskin (Viking)
　—watercolor

Year Award

1974 *Duffy and the Devil*
Retold by Harve Zemach;
Pictures by Margot Zemach
(Farrar)
—pen-and-ink drawings with
watercolor

1975 *Arrow to the Sun*
by Gerald McDermott (Viking)
—gouache and ink; black line
preseparated

1976 *Why Mosquitoes Buzz in People's
Ears*
by Verna Aardema; Pictures by
Leo and Diane Dillon (Dial)
—india ink; watercolor; pastels;
vellum and frisket masks

1977 *Ashanti to Zulu: African
Traditions*
by Margaret Musgrove;
Pictures by Leo and Diane
Dillon (Dial)
—pastels, watercolors, and
acrylics

Honor
Snow White and the Seven Dwarfs
Translated by Randall Jarrell;
Illustrated by Nancy Ekholm
Burkert (Farrar)
—brush and colored inks
When Clay Sings
by Byrd Baylor; Illustrated by
Tom Bahti (Scribner) (?)

Three Jovial Huntsmen
by Susan Jeffers (Bradbury)
—pen-and-ink drawings with
wash overlays painted in oils
Cathedral
by David Macaulay (Houghton)
—pen and ink

Jambo Means Hello
by Muriel Feelings; Illustrated
by Tom Feelings (Dial)
—graphite and paper collage

The Desert Is Theirs
by Byrd Baylor; Illustrated by
Peter Parnall (Scribner)
—pen and ink (?)
Strega Nona
Retold and illustrated by Tomie
de Paola (Prentice)
—watercolor and felt-tip pen
over graphite

The Amazing Bone
by William Steig (Farrar)
—watercolor (?)
The Contest
Retold and illustrated by Nonny
Hogrogian (Greenwillow)
—colored pencils and crayons for
full color; pencil drawings for
black and white
Fish for Supper
by M. B. Goffstein (Dial)
—ink drawings

Year Award

1978 *Noah's Ark*
by Peter Spier (Doubleday)
—F pencil on paper; watercolor
and white pencil; negatives
scratched

1979 *The Girl Who Loved Wild Horses*
by Paul Goble (Bradbury)
—full-color pen and ink and
watercolor

1980 *Ox-Cart Man*
by Donald Hall; Pictures by
Barbara Cooney (Viking)
—acrylics on gesso-coated board

1981 *Fables*
by Arnold Lobel (Harper)
—gouache and pencil

Honor
The Golem
by Beverly Brodsky McDermott
(Lippincott)
—gouache, watercolor, dye, and
ink
Hawk, I'm Your Brother
by Byrd Baylor; Illustrated by
Peter Parnall (Scribner)
—pen and ink (?)

Castle
by David Macaulay (Houghton)
—pen and ink
It Could Always Be Worse
Retold and illustrated by Margot
Zemach (Farrar)
—watercolor (?)

Freight Train
by Donald Crews (Greenwillow)
—preseparated art; airbrush
with transparent dyes
The Way to Start a Day
by Byrd Baylor; Illustrated by
Peter Parnall (Scribner)
—pen and ink (?)

Ben's Trumpet
by Rachel Isadora (Greenwillow)
—pen and ink
The Garden of Abdul Gasazi
by Chris Van Allsburg
(Houghton)
—carbon pencil on strathmore
paper
The Treasure
by Uri Shulevitz (Farrar)
—watercolor with black line on
acetate

The Bremen-Town Musicians
Retold and illustrated by Ilse
Plume (Doubleday)
—colored pencil and graphite (?)

Year Award

Honor

The Grey Lady and the Strawberry Snatcher
by Molly Bang (Four Winds)
—watercolor, sometimes with white gouache undercoat on gray construction paper

Mice Twice
by Joseph Low (McElderry/Atheneum)
—watercolor and pen and ink (?)

Truck
by Donald Crews (Greenwillow)
—four halftone separations with black line drawings

1982 *Jumanji*
by Chris Van Allsburg (Houghton)
—conté pencil with conté dust

Where the Buffaloes Begin
by Olaf Baker; Drawings by Stephen Gammell (Warne)
—pencil drawings (?)

On Market Street
by Arnold Lobel; Illustrated by Anita Lobel (Greenwillow)
—watercolor and pen and ink

Outside over There
by Maurice Sendak (Harper) (?)

A Visit to William Blake's Inn
by Nancy Willard; Illustrated by Alice and Martin Provensen (HBJ) (?)

1983 *Shadow*
by Blaise Cendrars; Translated and illustrated by Marcia Brown (Scribner)
—collage: paper, woodcuts, acrylics

A Chair for My Mother
by Vera Williams (Greenwillow)
—watercolor

When I Was Young in the Mountains
by Cynthia Rylant; Illustrated by Diane Goode (Dutton)
—watercolor and fine-colored pencil

1984 *The Glorious Flight: Across the Channel with Louis Blériot*
by Alice and Martin Provensen (Viking)
—acrylic and pen and ink

Little Red Riding Hood
Retold and illustrated by Trina Schart Hyman (Holiday House)
—ink and acrylic (?)

Year Award

1985 *Saint George and the Dragon*
Retold by Margaret Hodges;
Illustrated by Trina Schart
Hyman (Little, Brown)
—india ink and acrylic

1986 *The Polar Express*
by Chris Van Allsburg
(Houghton)
—full-color oil pastel on pastel
paper

1987 *Hey, Al*
by Arthur Yorinks; Illustrated by
Richard Egielski (Farrar)
—watercolor

1988 *Owl Moon*
by Jane Yolen;
Illustrated by John Schoenherr
(Philomel)
—pen and ink and watercolor

Honor
Ten, Nine, Eight
by Molly Bang (Greenwillow)
—gouache (poster paint)

Hansel and Gretel
Retold by Rika Lesser;
Illustrated by Paul O. Zelinsky
(Dodd)
—oil paintings
Have You Seen My Duckling?
by Nancy Tafuri (Greenwillow)
—watercolors and pastels
The Story of Jumping Mouse
Retold and illustrated by John
Steptoe (Lothrop)
—graphite pencil and india ink
on paper

The Relatives Came
by Cynthia Rylant; Illustrated by
Stephen Gammell (Bradbury)
—graphite and colored pencil
King Bidgood's in the Bathtub
by Audrey Wood; Illustrated by
Don Wood (HBJ)
—oil on pressed wood (?)

The Village of Round and Square Houses
by Ann Grifalconi (Little,
Brown)
—pastels (?)
Alphabatics
by Suse MacDonald (Bradbury)
—cells, vinyl acrylic; gouache
Rumpelstiltskin
Retold and illustrated by Paul
O. Zelinsky (Dutton)
—oil paintings

Mufaro's Beautiful Daughters
by John Steptoe (Lothrop)
—crosshatched pen and ink
and watercolor

Year Award

1989 *Song and Dance Man*
by Karen Ackerman;
Illustrated by Stephen Gammell
(Knopf)
—line drawings in colored pencil

1990 *Lon Po Po*
by Ed Young (Philomel)
—watercolor and pastels

Honor

The Boy of the Three-Year Nap
by Dianne Snyder;
Illustrated by Allen Say
(Houghton)
—brush-line, pen and ink, and
watercolor
Free Fall
by David Wiesner
(Lothrop)
—watercolor
Goldilocks and the Three Bears
by James Marshall (Dial)
—pen and ink and watercolor
Mirandy and Brother Wind
by Patricia C. McKissack;
Illustrated by Jerry Pinkney
(Knopf)
—pencil and watercolor

Bill Peet: An Autobiography
by Bill Peet (Houghton)
—pencil
Color Zoo
by Lois Ehlert (Lippincott)
—paper collage and die-
cut forms
*Hershel and the Hanukkah
Goblins*
by Eric Kimmel; Illustrated
by Trina Schart Hyman
(Holiday House)
—india ink and acrylic
paint
The Talking Eggs
by Robert San Souci;
Illustrated by Jerry Pinkney
(Dial)
—pencil, colored-pencil, and
watercolor

Year Award
1991 *Black and White*
   by David Macaulay (Houghton)
   "Seeing Things"—watercolor
   "Problem Parents"—ink line and wash
   "A Waiting Game"—watercolor and
      gouache
   "Udder Confusion"—gouache paint

Honor
*"More, More, More," Said the Baby: 3
   Love Stories*
   by Vera B. Williams
   (Greenwillow)
   —gouache paints; lettering
      painted in watercolor based on
   Gill Sans Extra Bold Print
Puss in Boots
   by Fred Marcellino
   (di Capua/Farrar)
   —colored pencil on taupe
   textured illustration paper

Some Useful Definitions

Acetate—a clear, plastic film used for overlays.

Airbrush—a mechanical painting tool that emits a fine spray of liquid or ink.

Batik—a wax-resistant process in which the design or image is first painted on
the surface in wax so that, when the surface is dyed, the wax sections will not
take the color.

Binder—the ingredient of a paint that holds together the particles of pigment and
fixes them into a continuous film as the paint dries.

Color preseparation—the process by which an artist prepares, manually, the art
to be printed in a four-, three-, or two-color book. This is done by preparing a
master preseparation and overlays, each specifying a color to be reproduced
for the image(s) contained in the area of the picture. When all of the overlays
are printed together, the colors form the final picture.

Conté pencil—square-sectioned drawing chalks in black, white, sanguine, and
sepia.

Dinobase—acetate sand-blasted to roughen the surface, making it similar to a
lithographic stone; no longer used.

Dye—a coloring agent soluble in liquid that imparts color to a surface by being
absorbed.

Engraving—any process by which a linear design is made on the surface of a
hard and durable substance.

F pencil—a medium-hard graphite pencil.

Four-color process—a printing process in which the full range of the colors of an
image is reproduced by means of four separate printing plates (black, blue,
red, and yellow), which can be separated via camera, computer, or artist.
After the separations, the plates are printed one on top of another in transparent process inks, as dictated by the separations, to create the final picture.

Frisket mask—a thin paper placed over an area not to be colored during painting
or airbrushing.

Graphite—a carbon in stick form used for drawing.

India ink—a permanent black ink made of lampblack and glue binder.

Linoleum cuts—a relief printing process in which the image or design is cut into the surface of a block of linoleum.

Lithograph—a print made by drawing on limestone or a zinc plate with a greasy material, then wetting the plate and applying greasy ink that will only adhere to the drawn line. Dampened paper is then rubbed over the stone with a special press to create the final print. A *lithographic crayon* or *pencil* is often used for drawing on the *lithographic stone*, which is a block of limestone with its surface ground so an image can be made upon it. In *offset lithography*, the image is first transferred to an intermediate surface (a rubber blanket) before it is transferred to the paper.

Overlay—a transparent or translucent film attached to artwork carrying additional detail to be reproduced.

Paint—a substance consisting of a pigment evenly dispersed in a liquid which, when applied to a surface as a fluid, dries into a continuous film of color. In *acrylic* paint, the pigment is dispersed in an emulsion binder that is a liquid form of acrylic resin. In *oil* paint, the pigment is dispersed in a drying oil (usually linseed). In *watercolor*, the finely ground pigment is dispersed in a water-soluble gum binder and is transparent; *gouache* is a watercolor that uses opaque rather than transparent colors; *tempera* is an opaque watercolor paint in which the pigment is ground in water and mixed with egg yolk; it can also be *poster paint*.

Pastels—a drawing medium consisting of pigment mixed with gum binder, rolled or compressed into stick form.

Pigment—a finely ground colored powder that may be mixed with a liquid vehicle to make paint.

Scratchboard—an ink technique in which a white board is covered with india ink and a design or image is scratched into it.

Wash—an application of ink or watercolor heavily diluted with water to form a thin film of transparent color.

Woodcut—a relief printing process in which the image or design is cut into the surface of a plank-grain wood block.

Bibliography

Children's Books: 1955-1957. New York: American Institute of Graphic Arts, 1957.

Children's Books: 1958-1960. New York: American Institute of Graphic Arts, 1958.

Children's Books: 1961-1962. New York: American Institute of Graphic Arts, 1962.

Ciancolo, Patricia J., ed. *Picture Books for Children.* American Library Assn., 1973.

de Angeli, Marguerite. *Butter at the Old Price.* Garden City: Doubleday, 1971.

Illustrations for Children: The Gladys English Collection. Sacramento: California Library Assn., Gladys English Memorial Collection Committee, 1963.

Jones, Helen. *Robert Lawson, Illustrator*. Boston: Little, 1972.

Kingman, Lee, and others. *Illustrators of Children's Books, 1957-1966*. Boston: Horn Book, 1968.

Kingman, Lee, ed. *Newbery and Caldecott Medal Books: 1956-1965*. Boston: Horn Book, 1965.

Kingman, Lee, ed. *Newbery and Caldecott Medal Books: 1966-1975*. Boston: Horn Book, 1975.

Kingman, Lee, ed. *Newbery and Caldecott Medal Books: 1976-1985*. Boston: Horn Book, 1986.

Lanes, Selma G. *The Art of Maurice Sendak*. New York: Abrams, 1980.

Larkin, David, ed. *The Art of Nancy Ekholm Burkert*. New York: Harper, 1977.

Lucie-Smith, Edward. *The Thames and Hudson Dictionary of Art Terms*. London: Thames & Hudson, 1984.

Martin, Judy. *The Longman Dictionary of Art*. Harlow, Eng.: Longman Group, 1986.

Miller, Bertha Mahony, and others. *Caldecott Medal Books: 1938-1957*. Boston: Horn Book, 1957.

Quick, John. *Artists' and Illustrators' Encyclopedia, II ed*. New York: McGraw-Hill, 1977.

Shulevitz, Uri. *Writing with Pictures*. New York: Watson-Guptill, 1985.

Viguers, Ruth Hill, and others. *Illustrators of Children's Books, 1946-1956*. Boston: Horn Book, 1958.

Also consulted: all issues of *Horn Book Magazine*: 1938-1986.

Author/Illustrator Index

Title Index